A RETURN TO COMMON SENSE

SEVEN BOLD WAYS TO REVITALIZE DEMOCRACY

MICHAEL WALDMAN

BRENNAN CENTER FOR JUSTICE

SOURCEBOOKS, INC.®
NAPERVILLE, ILLINOIS

This publication is designed to provide accurate and authoritative information in regard to the subject matter covered. It is sold with the understanding that the publisher is not engaged in rendering legal, accounting, or other professional service. If legal advice or other expert assistance is required, the services of a competent professional person should be sought.—From a Declaration of Principles Jointly Adopted by a Committee of the American Bar Association and a Committee of Publishers and Associations

Published by Sourcebooks, Inc.
P.O. Box 4410, Naperville, Illinois 60567-4410
(630) 961-3900
Fax: (630) 961-2168
www.sourcebooks.com

Library of Congress Cataloging-in-Publication Data

Waldman, Michael.
  A return to common sense : 7 bold reforms you can make to save our failed government / Michael Waldman.
       p. cm.
  Includes bibliographical references.
  1. United States—Politics and government. I. Title.
JK274.W235 2008
 324.60973—dc22

                          2008006726

          Printed and bound in the United States of America.
              BG 10 9 8 7 6 5 4 3 2 1

ALSO BY MICHAEL WALDMAN

My Fellow Americans
Sourcebooks, 2003

POTUS Speaks
Simon & Schuster, 2000

Who Robbed America?
Random House, 1990

Big Business Reader, 2nd ed. (ed., with Mark Green)
Pilgrim, 1984

Who Runs Congress?, 4th ed. (with Mark Green)
Dell, 1983

To my colleagues at the Brennan Center for Justice,
who challenge and inspire me, and to
Liz, Ben, Susannah, and Joshua

CONTENTS

A NOTE FROM
THE AUTHOR

We are months from an historic national election, the first since 1952 without an incumbent president or vice-president on the ballot. The Republican president's approval ratings hover only slightly above those of the Democratic Congress. We face enormous challenges, stretching well beyond our borders. They are dwarfed only by our seeming inability to meet them.

I served at the top levels of American government, as Bill Clinton's chief speechwriter and his top aide on political reform. I worked in the White House for nearly seven years. Around my neck, I wore the blue White House pass coveted by generations of young strivers. Now I lead the Brennan Center for Justice at NYU School of Law, a think tank and advocacy group focused on democracy and justice.

With that background, I write this book with a mixture of hope and urgency. It is clear to me that we can meet the challenges we face. It is less clear to me that we *will*.

A RETURN TO COMMON SENSE

I firmly believe that Americans have the intelligence, the creativity, and the moral integrity to address global warming, terrorism, health care, and economic uncertainty. I am equally certain that we no longer enjoy a mechanism through which to do so. To meet these challenges we need more than ample resources. Today, government is broken. This volume explores seven ways we can begin to move forward, to renew our government, and to reconnect it to the people for whom it was formed. My core thesis is this: If we want to solve our problems, we must fix our systems.

Despite the country's many challenges, this is an exciting time. Plainly there is an intense hunger for civic engagement. At this moment, we can still act—if we are strong enough to transcend partisan rancor and put deep democracy reforms at the core of a new approach to politics.

Michael Waldman
December 2007

INTRODUCTION

In early 1776, Thomas Paine published *Common Sense.* That celebrated book put forward the radical idea that government depends for its legitimacy entirely on the consent of the governed. The Declaration of Independence, published a few months later, could simply have broken with Britain, but it did far more. It set out a vision of equal opportunity and political self-governance, one plainly at odds with reality in that revolutionary year.

For two centuries our history has been marked by an effort to live out the meaning of that creed—never easily, and at every step, always over fierce opposition.[1] In the era of Andrew Jackson in the 1830s, men without property won the right to vote. In the Civil War and after, political rights and civic freedom were won by the slaves, only to be taken from them in a brutal repression. In the Progressive Era of the early 1900s, we began to use government as an effective tool to counter excessive economic power—assuring that democracy would not be overwhelmed by a new aristocracy. Women won the vote, in effect doubling the franchise. Then the New Deal not only stretched a safety net through programs like Social Security, but created new institutions to vest political power in a larger group of hands, by protecting the right to organize unions. And in the civil rights era of the 1950s and 1960s, we sharply expanded the circle of democracy again, with African Americans and then millions of others gaining long-denied legal equality.

At each moment, those who opposed wider democracy worried that giving more power to more people would lead to lassitude, a dilution of American character, or a government so bloated and voracious that it would sap entrepreneurial spirit. At every step, they were proven wrong. Each loosening of the vise expanded the nation's creative and commercial spirit. We learned that our country grows stronger when power is entrusted to more hands.

For Americans, democracy isn't just another in a laundry list of issues. It is *the* issue—and it always has been.

But today, we see dangerous signs that our democracy, instead of rising, is in retreat. We boast the world's oldest representative government, yet in many years barely half of all Americans vote. (In France, in 2007, it was a *scandale* when turnout fell to 85 percent. By the most authoritative measure, our voter turnout ranks near the bottom of industrial democracies.[2]) The United States imposes the most onerous voter registration rules in the West. Political campaigns are awash in some $5 billion dollars in privately raised funds.[3] This absurd system forces candidates to spend so much time fundraising they have little time to tend to the public business. Few legislative elections are even faintly competitive, thanks in part to computer-aided partisan gerrymandering. The number of Washington lobbyists has tripled in a decade, overwhelmingly representing commercial concerns, paralyzing Congress and ensuring that policy tilts toward narrow interests and the wealthy. And all the while, in the wake of September 11th, the historic balance of power among government branches has tilted badly off kilter, with power authority surging to the presidency, and the White House claiming unprecedented constitutional authority to act above the law and beyond the reach of the courts.

American democracy, once the envy of the world, urgently needs repair. Our capacity to solve problems languishes, yet the need to do so compounds. Lawmakers should grapple with long-postponed challenges, such as climate change or health care—yet if they do, narrow interests and the forces of stasis will inevitably combine to make needed action nearly impossible. This combination raises deep questions about whether our government and political system can face hard challenges.

The perilous state of our government and democracy drives the creation of this book. *A Return to Common Sense* looks at the institutions of American self-government. It shows where they are broken. And it proposes ways to fix them—concrete, specific steps we could take that would make government listen more and work better. Thomas

Paine relied, he told his readers, on "simple facts, plain arguments, and common sense." So do we.

★ ★ ★

Of course, worries about corrupt politicians and apathetic voters have long been the background noise of American life. It was Mark Twain, not Jon Stewart, who quipped, "There is no native criminal class except Congress." But something has changed, for the worse. Our accumulating troubles have begun to feed on one another. According to a Gallup Poll, trust in government has plummeted to historic low levels, last seen during Watergate.[4] Citizens understand that government fails in basic tasks not because politicians are more venal (they aren't), or because voters are less intelligent (we're better educated than a half century ago, albeit not about civics), but because too often the machinery of democracy and government is dysfunctional.

That's the bad news. The good news is that specific reforms can go far to revitalize American democracy. Developed in states and cities, based on trial and error and experience, they are powered by the new political energy seen in recent campaigns and on the Internet. Plainly, a growing sense of public engagement and civic energy is building that can help renew democracy, if we make sure that broken institutions don't get in the way.

First, we must fix our voting system. To a startling degree, this irreducible tool of self-governance has been blunted by inattention or outright voter suppression.

Americans have a chance to build a modern election system that—for the first time in our history—actually encourages citizens to vote. We can move to universal voter registration, with government taking the responsibility to make sure that all eligible citizens can participate. We can improve elections in other ways, including national standards to stop disenfranchisement of eligible voters. And we can ensure security and accuracy in the network of new electronic voting machines. The goal must be that everyone who wants to register, can register; everyone who wants to vote, can vote; and every vote that is cast is a vote that is counted.

Then, we must renew our political system—recognizing that elections today are rigged to diminish competition and deny citizens their role. This goes beyond campaign finance reform, though the mad dash for cash continues to corrupt our government. Redistricting reform to inject competition into Congress, and an end to the Electoral College to greatly broaden competition in presidential campaigns, will go far toward making every vote count.

Finally, the government itself needs repair. This project will require many years of work. Those who hold power at both ends of Pennsylvania Avenue must recognize that constitutionally grounded rules of conduct are not just a nuisance, but are necessary for the effective functioning of American government. Thus, concrete steps to restore checks and balances and the rule of law must be part of the renewal of democratic institutions.

All these changes require leadership from lawmakers and those who seek office. But we cannot expect government to reform itself. Citizens must build a long-term movement for democracy reform. Our goal, in all of this, is a political system that is far more participatory, more accountable, and more responsive than it is today. We seek to restore the "feedback loop" connecting government and citizens.

★ ★ ★

We must begin to focus on democracy reforms right now, while eyes are drawn to politics and the high stakes are evident. A few of these changes can still be made before Election Day. If that happens, the 2008 election will be fairer, more accurate, and more accountable than it would otherwise be. Even more, we can insist that our political leaders focus on the steps needed to renew democracy as they seek our votes. We can make sure that *after* the ballots are counted, issues of institutional reform don't simply recede to the background, relegated to the bin of arcane process concerns. Fixing our public institutions should be high on the agenda for the next crop of political leaders. Changes should be made quickly. If they are, the next president and Congress will have a chance—not a guarantee, but a chance—to govern in the national interest.

Let's be clear: Both parties deserve blame for the flaws in American democracy. Both grab for power through naked gerrymandering. At key moments in the fight for campaign reform, too many lawmakers act more as members of the Incumbency Party rather than as

Democrats or Republicans. (In one major area, however, there is a sharp difference among parties. For much of our history, Democrats blocked voting rights, using the Black Codes and Jim Crow laws to suppress the votes of large numbers of African Americans in the South. Today, though, it is Republicans who have sponsored nearly all the recent bills stiffening voter ID requirements; only one president, George W. Bush, has emphasized prosecution of voter fraud in battleground states. Those are facts.)

Reform works only when a broad segment of both parties rallies toward it. A push for a strong democracy can help to fill a hole at the center of our politics. Every policy proposal has embedded within it a moral vision—a sense of how people think and act, what drives them, singly and in families and communities. Conservative politics for decades has revolved around a highly individualized notion, denigrating the role of government, but that vision appears to have run its course, far less powerful an answer to the challenges of a threatening twenty-first century. Liberals, in turn, too often have seemed a collection of constituencies, held together (at times) by charismatic politicians or appealing but shopworn policy proposals. There is, in short, a crying need for a revitalized progressive public philosophy that helps guide not only what laws are passed but how we can revive ourselves as a great and thriving nation.

Democracy holds that ordinary citizens are the source of legitimacy for their government, and that they are best off governing themselves. That—as we would say in the digital age—the "distributed intelligence" of numerous individuals is better than the blinkered resolve of a centralized "decider." Economists, too, talk about the "wisdom of crowds."[5] If progressives can once again tap that notion of ordinary citizens as the agents of their own progress, they can touch hearts—something that reams of position papers simply will not do. There's a charisma of ideas—ideas that can mobilize people by offering a different vision of the good society. We can overwhelm the power of entrenched money and narrow interest with the volume of new participants in the political process.

So let's look at the ways we can fix America's democratic institutions. New policies aren't enough. We need to make the changes that can make all the other changes possible. We should listen to Al Smith, a child of the Lower East Side who rose to governor of New York State. "The only cure for the ills of democracy," he said, "is more democracy."

Seven Steps to Revitalize Democracy

Institute universal voter registration. Every American adult citizen should be able to vote, period. That will require a shift in how we see this most basic right, and a new system for registering voters.

Establish national standards to stop disenfranchisement. We must overhaul our quaintly chaotic system of running elections, ranging from how we make voter lists to changing Election Day itself.

Fix electronic voting. We should move beyond the "hanging chads" of yore and the suspiciously hackable electronic voting machines of today to institute a modern, auditable system for counting votes.

Create fair elections through public funding. We can free candidates from the tyranny of fundraising and boost the power of millions of citizens who give small amounts to the candidates they support.

Move to popular election for the president of the United States. Two centuries after we kicked out King George III, it's time to actually give voters the job of electing the chief executive. Fortunately, there is an innovative way to do this without waiting for a constitutional amendment.

Restore competitive elections by ending gerrymandering. We should take redistricting away from the cartel of incumbent politicians of both parties, who have an obvious stake in drawing lines to stay in office, to increase dramatically the number of genuinely contested elections.

Restore checks and balances. We should curb the Imperial Presidency by restoring habeas corpus, a nine-hundred-year-old protection written into the Constitution, which has been discarded in the fight against terrorism. We should reinvigorate congressional oversight. We should restore independence and professionalism to key government agencies such as the Department of Justice.

FIXING THE VOTE

PART ONE: FIXING THE VOTE

"The right to vote freely for the candidate of one's choice is of the essence of a democratic society, and any restrictions on that right strike at the heart of representative government."—Chief Justice Earl Warren, Reynolds v. Sims[6]

Voting is the heart of democracy. For many years, it seemed we had long ago settled who could vote and how their votes would be counted. On Election Night, the machinery of democracy appeared neutral and precise. Now, of course, we know differently. We smile cynically along with William Magear ("Boss") Tweed, who said in the 1860s, "As long as I count the votes, what are you going to do about it?" Yet that's really unacceptable, so many years later. So the first step to fix our democracy must be a national drive to create a modern and effective election system, in which we finally give life to the promise that every American can vote.

Would it really matter if we improve the way we vote? Consider the recent string of breathtakingly close elections. Of course, in 2000 George W. Bush's margin in Florida was 537 votes. But that wasn't even the narrowest victory. Al Gore won New Mexico by less, and Iowa, Wisconsin, and Oregon each were decided by less than 7,000 ballots. Four years later, when Bush won the popular vote comfortably, Wisconsin, New Hampshire, and New Mexico were decided by less than 12,000 votes each. Control of the U.S. Senate wobbled for two days in 2006 until Virginia and Montana swung to the Democrats by a few thousand votes out of millions cast. In the House in 2006, one seat was decided by 91 votes, and another by 369.[7]

Those microscopic margins are dwarfed by the volume of votes lost due to disenfranchisement, voting machine errors, ineptitude, and chicanery. In 2000, according to the most authoritative study, millions of would-be voters were turned away due to problems with registration and voter lists.[8] Today, after years of fitful reform, even larger numbers of potential votes are simply never cast due to obstacles still in place. An additional 1.5 million would be added to the rolls if the "Motor Voter" law to register people at government offices was enforced only as much as it was a decade ago. Nearly four million citizens with felony convictions could regain the right to vote when they leave prison. At least nine million more could be expected to cast ballots if they could register when they vote, as is now allowed in several states. And if the worst voter ID proposals become law, such as those requiring a government document with a current address, we know that at least twenty-one million citizens lack the documentation they would need to vote.

The 2000 Florida fiasco surprised most Americans. Less excusable is the halfhearted progress we have made since. In response to the mess, in 2002 Congress passed a new voter law, the Help America Vote Act (HAVA).[9] In some respects, this measure is making things better. But the new law only scrapes the surface of the worst problems. With fifty states each required to implement changes, this, too, has created huge opportunities for mischief and abuse. If we are going to fix voting, we'll have to think big and go deep. Let's look at some key reforms.

1

END VOTER REGISTRATION AS WE KNOW IT

Universal Registration— What's So Hard About That?

Why do so few Americans vote? We are not a nation of slackers, yet voter turnout rates consistently rank near the bottom of all democracies. In the United States, a typical off-year election sees turnout at 47 percent. Even in a presidential race, in recent years roughly four out of ten voting-age citizens haven't made it to the polls.[10] Turnout is rising somewhat, but it still lags far behind that of other countries.

Social scientists routinely dissect the electorate to find reasons for our habitually low turnout. Explanations range from disillusionment with government and weak political parties to fraying bonds of civic engagement, such as the decline in labor unions, political party clubs, fraternal organizations, and even, as Robert Putnam has pointed out, bowling leagues.[11] This is all true, but insufficient to explain the phenomenon.

The fact is, most people who are registered actually do show up to vote. In 2004, nearly nine of ten who were registered cast a ballot. That's true across racial and ethnic lines. Both whites and blacks voted at almost the same rate, if they were registered in the first place. But roughly one quarter of eligible citizens is not registered, and the rates of registration vary.[12] If you want to ask where the voters are, you have to start by asking where the *registered* voters are. Significantly, our Byzantine voter laws keep many people from registering, and thus from voting. These are laws we can and must change.

Why do we have voter registration?

As a hoary southern saying has it, "When you see a turtle on a fence post, it didn't get there by accident." We are still governed by the restrictive registration system first put in place a century ago to stop certain European immigrants and former slaves from voting. Former presidents Jimmy Carter and Gerald Ford headed a commission that concluded, "The registration laws in force throughout the United States are among the world's most demanding … [and are] one reason why voter turnout in the United States is near the bottom of the developed world."[13] The obstacles to participation weren't put there "by accident."

At the time of Lexington and Concord, laws sharply limited who could vote: only whites, only men, and only property owners, which meant roughly six out of ten white men. Raucous debates over who could vote roiled the newly independent colonies. John Adams, for his part, drafted a constitution for Massachusetts that limited voting only to taxpaying property owners. Benjamin Franklin and Thomas

Paine, on the other hand, led the fight to abolish property requirements in Pennsylvania. Franklin wrote scathingly:

> *Today a man owns a jackass worth fifty dollars and he is entitled to vote; but before the next election the jackass dies. The man in the mean time has become more experienced, his knowledge of the principles of government, and his acquaintance with mankind, are more extensive, and he is therefore better qualified to make a proper selection of rulers—but the jackass is dead and the man cannot vote. Now gentlemen, pray inform me, in whom is the right of suffrage? In the man or in the jackass?*[14]

Over the next half century, the new country surged westward. Bewigged aristocrats no longer defined its political culture. After 1824, when Andrew Jackson of Tennessee won the most votes but lost the presidency in the House of Representatives, his supporters organized to change voting laws by removing property restrictions, and swept him into power. Turnout nearly tripled in four years to 78 percent. By the 1850s, property requirements as a precondition to voting were gone almost entirely. The United States began to move closer toward a wide and participatory democracy.

The next great struggle was over race. Lincoln's "new birth of freedom" proclaimed more than an end to slavery. The drafters of the Fourteenth Amendment to the Constitution, which guarantees "equal protection of the law," intended it to be a charter for civic and social equality.[15] Four years later, the Fifteenth Amendment guaranteed "the right to vote" to freed male slaves and their descendents. In Mississippi, Louisiana, and other southern states, freedmen and Republicans elected governments backed by former slaves. Two African Americans served as U.S. senators, and there were fifteen black congressmen.[16]

Then came a brutal backlash. In a deal to settle the disputed 1876 presidential election, the U.S. Army withdrew from the Old Confederacy. The South's "redemption" snatched away the voting rights of millions of U.S. citizens.[17] After the populists of the 1890s briefly threatened to create a cross-racial coalition of blacks and white farmers and workers, the local power structure passed Jim Crow laws such as the poll tax, literacy tests for voting, and felony disenfranchisement. On their face the laws applied to everyone, but in fact they were carefully crafted to freeze out African Americans. In Louisiana, in 1896, 130,000 blacks were registered to vote; by 1904, the number had plummeted to 1,342.[18]

Meanwhile in the North, civic leaders pushed similar measures to restrict the vote—aimed not at former slaves but at millions of new European immigrants who were eligible to vote. The overt goal was to keep Tammany Hall and other political clubs from corruptly marshalling the Irish and Italian immigrants now passing through Ellis Island and swelling the cities. The underlying purpose was to keep those immigrants from voting at all. New York State, for example, required voter registration solely in New York City, not the rest of the largely rural Empire State. John Adams's great-grandson warned that universal suffrage would mean "the government of ignorance and vice—it means a European, and especially Celtic, proletariat on the Atlantic coast; an African proletariat on the shores of the Gulf; and a Chinese proletariat on the Pacific."[19]

These two pushes, against voting by blacks and European immigrants, helped lead to the voter registration system still largely in effect. We have come to take it for granted that voter registration is natural and inevitable, when it is in fact an obstacle course—one designed to be maneuvered successfully only by "worthy" citizens.

For half a century, a combination of law, vigilantism, and police power kept the circle of voting tight. The Constitution granted women the right to vote in 1918. But south of the Mason Dixon line, blacks were effectively prevented from voting—until the dramatic victories of the civil rights movement in the 1960s. The Voting Rights Act of 1965, won with the fortitude and lives of marchers in Selma and elsewhere, amounted to a political revolution. All through the South, black vote participation rates skyrocketed.

By the end of the twentieth century, it seemed, the long struggle to expand the franchise to every adult American had been won.

In fact, this was not the case. Millions of voters now face a silent disenfranchisement—for reasons ranging from incompetence to racist intimidation. Instead of billy clubs and literacy tests, the means for blocking access to the ballot are more likely found in obscure government offices, dense regulations, and a far-ranging media campaign designed to create the conditions for more disenfranchisement.

The silent disenfranchisement takes many forms. In a country where one in six Americans moves in a year, government does not routinely keep such people registered to vote, even if they stay in their own state. Harvard political scientist Thomas Patterson notes that two-thirds of nonvoters in 2000 were ineligible to vote because they hadn't registered. "Of these, one in three was a former registered voter who had moved and hadn't re-registered." [20] When you put in a change-of-address notice, it doesn't routinely go to the voter registration clerk.

Millions of voters routinely are knocked off the voter rolls for one reason or another, and often are not told about it. A rash of voter ID laws adds to the confusion; on Election Day in 2006, a governor, two members of Congress, and a secretary of state in charge of voting were turned away for failing to show the proper paperwork. And in most states, voters must remember to register nearly a month before Election Day—before the series of presidential debates, for example. As campaign professionals will confirm, many voters often do not truly focus in on races until after the World Series ends, in other words, after it is too late to register.

Government is supposed to do more, but has been half-hearted at best. In 1993 President Clinton signed the National Voter Registration Act (NVRA). Under the "Motor Voter" law, as it is popularly known, state Departments of Motor Vehicles, welfare centers, and other offices are supposed to register voters. At first the law was enforced. By 1996, government agencies were registering 2.6 million voters a year. More recently, enforcement by these bureaucracies had dropped by nearly two-thirds. An investigation by three voter rights groups found some offices where no forms were given out at all.[21] If state governments shook off that torpor and enforced the law only as enthusiastically as a decade ago, millions could be registered.

Piecemeal reforms have merit. It is certainly important to make sure that Election Day does not dissolve into bedlam. But we will miss a key opportunity if that is all we do. Our entire notion of voter registration needs rethinking. We should recognize that voting is a right, not a privilege. We should recognize that individuals ought not be charged with figuring out how to register and stay registered. And we should commit to the idea that in a democracy, the government has a duty, moral and legal, to make it possible for every eligible citizen to be able to vote.

Here are some ways to do just that.

UNIVERSAL VOTER REGISTRATION

One reform could transform our democracy. It's time to end voter registration as we know it. Our great goal should be a system of universal voter registration, in which every eligible citizen is able to vote, period. The government should be responsible for registering voters and keeping the list.

Every election, campaigns and nonprofit organizations spend hundreds of millions of dollars to register voters. This cycle repeats every two or four years, all at a time when government keeps numerous databases and lists of adult Americans. We don't privatize most other key roles in our functioning democracy. We don't tell people to organize themselves to show up for the census, or to collect taxes. We don't ask litigants to rustle up a jury pool. We see all these as government's natural, obvious obligation. We should also see government as having the prime role in creating an accurate list of who can vote, too. Steven Hill of the New America Foundation estimates that universal voter registration could add fifty million Americans to the rolls.[22]

Universal registration could be achieved several different ways. One plan, possibly the best, would have the government create a new, universal voter list. In Canada, for example, the federal government built a permanent national voter register in 1997 by going door to door to find voters. The government updates that list every election year through mass mailings that remind voters to update their address information if it is wrong. In addition, taxpayers are given a box to check on returns asking if they would like to be registered, new citizens are asked if they would like to register to vote, and the elections authority receives information on changes in address or other information from Canada Post and various federal, provincial, territorial, and municipal agencies. Officials also add to the list by culling from auto registrations and local voter lists. The list is augmented by door-to-door canvassers focused on young people and those in mobile homes. Finally, voters can also register themselves, either in advance or on Election Day. In all, 94 percent of adult Canadians make the list. Nearly 10 percent more of the voting-age population votes in the Great White North than here.[23] And it's not just Canada; in

Great Britain, voters register voluntarily just as we do here. But the government then follows up with a household survey, sending people door to door to make sure nobody has been missed (just as in the U.S. Census).[24]

We know that government could do this here in the United States, even today. Cities and towns in Massachusetts have run an annual state census for two hundred years. Every year in Boston, mail surveys go out to every citizen over the age of 18 who lives within city limits, asking for current address information. If a household doesn't respond to the survey, canvassers go door to door to make sure they get everyone in the city on the census list. This list is considered accurate; it is even used to call people for jury duty. Why can't we use this method to register every eligible citizen to vote?

Another approach would call for the government to piece together the voter rolls through other existing lists. The federal government already has selective service lists of every eighteen-year-old male, Social Security numbers for all workers, and numerous other tallies. It could patch together a highly accurate voter roll from those partial lists.

In crafting such a system, we run up against two deeply ingrained traditions of American governance, and, indeed, the American political personality: localism and libertarianism.

In the United States, often we think that it's better to scatter responsibility among local governments than to risk a heavy hand from Washington. Today's voting system, of course, is stubbornly federalist, with responsibilities and roles overlapping among local governments, states, and the national government. Errors are inevitable. More, we live in a mobile and increasingly homogenized society; about one in eight Americans moves out of state between presidential elections. If we really want to create a working, government-run voter list, we will have to decide if it is run by Washington, D.C., or fifty state capitals.

One can imagine the arguments on both sides. The states have run voting since the country's founding. Existing systems are already in place. It would be, the argument would go, a severe encroachment of federal power—possibly even requiring a constitutional amendment. There's no reason to think that the federal government, potentially at far remove from the voters, would manage such a system well, and any policy or design errors would be magnified. On the other hand, the record of many state governments on issues ranging from electronic voting to voter lists—let alone partisan firebombs like voter ID—does not inspire confidence. A federal list would be more cost efficient. Still, it may better recognize reality to leave the listmaking where it is now, in the states, subject to a strong national standard. Setting up a system like this will be hard, and will undoubtedly involve trial and error. This may be a case when Justice Louis Brandeis's timeworn notion of states as "laboratories of democracy" may be true.

At the same time, our ornery libertarian streak—which resists governmental intrusion and hates to be told what to do—suggests citizens should have the chance to "opt out." The Supreme Court has held that voter registration is speech, and might rule that declining to register is also a form of expression.[25] Allowing an opt-out choice probably wouldn't be that hard, and would potentially minimize an otherwise potent strain of opposition to a new voter registration system.

A list created by the government would have the advantage of being far harder to scam. Those worried about voter fraud would know that the government had taken the responsibility to create the ultimate list. In urging a system of universal registration, the New America Foundation, a centrist think tank, sets out the terms of the "grand bargain." "It's the best way to bring together conservatives concerned about fraud in elections and liberals concerned about low voter registration. We need a coherent system that ensures all of us can vote, but none of us can vote more than once."[26]

We could take steps that would move toward universal registration immediately. We could, for example, preregister every high school student at age sixteen (so they are ready to vote when they turn eighteen). With the new electronic databases required under the federal voter law, citizens who remain in their home state could stay registered throughout a lifetime without having to reregister again and again each time they move. We could automatically register citizens who pay taxes, though using the IRS for purposes other than tax-raising poses potential privacy concerns. Possibly the chance to "opt out" of registering could be a box to check on the 1040 tax form (although grumpy citizens might vent their pique at Uncle Sam by saying no to voting).

The most significant step toward universal registration already exists and works well in several states: Election Day registration.

NEXT BEST THING: ELECTION DAY REGISTRATION

Eight states have already taken a key step toward universal voter registration by allowing voters to register on Election Day. You show up at a polling place, present some identification, you are registered—and you can vote. Minnesota, Maine, and Wisconsin instituted Election Day registration in the 1970s. Idaho, New Hampshire, and Wyoming did so a decade later. Montana passed it in 2006, in time for the midterm election; Iowa followed the next year. Nearly 4,000 Montanans registered on Election Day, more than the margin of victory for new Senator Jon Tester. In 2007, North Carolina instituted "same day" registration—voters can register any day during the early voting period two weeks before Election Day (but not the day itself).

Election Day registration (EDR) turbocharges turnout. Most estimates show it boosts voting by 5 to 7 percent. [27] In addition, allowing voters to register while casting a ballot simply sweeps away many bureaucratic cobwebs associated with voter lists. If a voter shows up at the polls, and her name isn't on the list, she won't be turned away, and generally does not have to worry about provisional ballots or other patchwork solutions. She simply registers on the spot. States with EDR have fewer problems with registration lists on Election Day than is typical. There is no evidence of increased fraud or chicanery.[28]

So what are the arguments against EDR? Local election officials, for one, fret that hordes of tardy voters will turn up at polling places, threatening chaos. Some voters simply don't bother to register in advance, figuring they will just show up if they feel like it on Election Day. Election agency bureaucrats brandish stories of long lines stretching into the night, and worry about cost and management. But Minnesota officials—who are used to doing it this way— rightly insist that everyone calm down.

A greater obstacle is the cadre of incumbent politicians who worry that Election Day registration can upset their settled plans. In 1998 a surge of young voters elected former pro-wrestler Jesse "The Body" Ventura, an independent, as governor of Minnesota. Ventura barely showed in the polls for much of the race. But under Minnesota law, he qualified for limited public financing, and in debate he outshone the tepid Republican and Democratic-Farmer-Labor candidates. (One letter to the editor put it, "Jesse speaks English." The others "speak politician."[29]) Remarkably, one in six voters registered on Election Day. Reported the *Washington Monthly:* "Anoka County, a populous suburban area north of Minneapolis, provides a striking example of the Ventura effect. There, Jesse received 51 percent of the vote (compared to 37 percent statewide). Turnout in the county was an astounding 72 percent, with 22,375 people registering on Election Day."[30] All told "The Body" wrestled some 250,000 bodies to the polls.

Most exciting, this reform forces candidates and parties to shift their strategies toward "people power." At present, campaigns fillet the electorate into carpaccio-thin slices: soccer moms, office park dads, gun magazine readers, and so on—a refined and expensive process. Candidates don't waste time or money trying to woo the disaffected or shake the torpor of nonvoters. Election Day registration gives campaigns the chance for a different strategy: persuade and mobilize a wide audience. There is always a risk that last-minute dirty tricks, gutter charges, or sheer emotionalism could play a bigger role than today. But such passions are hardly the product of the Internet age alone. In 1884, Republican James G. Blaine was leading the presidential race. A week before the election, he attended a rally where a minister denounced the Democrats as the party of "rum, Romanism and rebellion." The slur triggered massive Catholic turnout in New York City, which delivered the presidency to Grover Cleveland.[31]

No, carefully packaged grey-flannel politicians have more to fear from the fact that voter enthusiasm suddenly matters more. Passion can drive turnout. That, in turn, would create an electoral cycle in which wider participation will lead to deeper reform. More voters can be the first key factor to winning numerous other needed changes in government.

An Ugly Remnant of Jim Crow

A surprisingly large number—five million American citizens—still are legally barred from voting due to a felony conviction.[32] Four out of five of those disenfranchised are out of prison or never served a day of time. As former president Bill Clinton has said, "When you've done your time and are back in the community, working, paying taxes, trying to raise a family and lead a good life—it's an abomination that we deny the right to vote."[33]

Over the past two decades, our laws have deemed more and more things to be criminal, which swelled the ranks of the disenfranchised. Since 1980 the prison population in the United States has doubled. The number of those in prison due to drug offenses rose tenfold.[34] Today a larger share of American adults is disenfranchised due to felony conviction than at any point in American history.[35]

Most felony disenfranchisement laws were enacted after the Civil War.[36] The statutes targeted crimes such as "vagrancy" or "miscegenation" that were seen as likely to be committed by blacks. Mississippi's State Supreme Court explained this was perfectly acceptable, since the African American community's "criminal members [are] given rather to furtive offenses than to the robust crimes of the whites," supposedly red-blooded crimes such as murder and rape.[37] Carter

Glass, later a prominent Democratic U.S. senator, assured Virginia's constitutional convention in 1901 that felony disenfranchisement would "eliminate the darkey as a political factor in this state in less than five years." Virginia's law is still in effect. Today one in four black men there is barred from voting.

Shouldn't criminals be punished? Of course. But when they return to society, we ought not stamp a scarlet "F" on their foreheads. Managing the reentry of the 600,000 people who leave prison every year is a major social challenge. We want them integrated into the community, bound to its norms and rules in every way possible. As President George W. Bush said in his 2003 State of the Union, "America is the land of the second chance, and when the gates of the prison open, the path ahead should lead to a better life."[38] That's why Prison Fellowship founder Charles Colson and former Rep. Jack Kemp, as well as numerous law enforcement professionals, have joined the call for change.

This movement has achieved surprising results. In the last decade, sixteen states have reformed their laws. Iowa Governor Tom Vilsack ended permanent disenfranchisement by executive order, and Rhode Island voters passed a constitutional amendment restoring voting rights to citizens the day they leave prison. Most significant, Florida Governor Charlie Crist, a Republican elected in 2006, also moved to end felony disenfranchisement by executive action. Some of his cabinet members were aghast and sought to block it. "The time is now for us to do what is right," Crist told them. "I believe in simple human justice and that when somebody has paid their debt to society, it is paid in full. There's a time to move on, a time to give them an opportunity to have redemption."[39] Crist largely prevailed. People convicted of most felonies can have their voting rights restored without a clemency hearing. Florida's process is still far from automatic or complete, and many eligible voters may never learn their rights have been restored. Still, the move could lead to restored voting rights for hundreds of thousands.

2

ROCKING THE VOTE

Fixing Voter Lists and Election Day

Even if we create universal registration, we will run up against obstacles that keep many eligible voters away from the polls. Some of this disenfranchisement is accidental, the product of slipshod election administration. Some has to do with the way we run Election Day itself. But too much is deliberate, the product of a concerted public relations campaign to require government-issued ID cards to vote.

As we learned in 2000, election administration was an afterthought. Ballot design varied from county to county. Even today, election administration is hardly a sleek machine. Officials operate under inadequate conflict-of-interest rules. Some are openly partisan. Katherine Harris of Florida and J. Kenneth Blackwell of Ohio chaired their state party presidential drives while supposedly refereeing the contest. Blackwell oversaw elections while he himself ran for governor. Election officials are bombarded by lobbyists for voting machine companies, auditing firms, and others, with few safeguards to assure that contracting decisions are made on what you do, not who you know or whose campaign you backed. The 13,000 separate jurisdictions that administer elections vary wildly in skill and neutrality. Information and voter lists must be parceled out to at least 200,000 separate polling places across the country.[40]

Election Day in Ohio in 2004 was a Petri dish in which all the ills of election administration were stirred together. Voters in Cleveland, Toledo, and Cincinnati, mostly in inner-city neighborhoods, waited up to ten hours outside polling places. Students at Kenyon College waited five hours in the rain. Apparently there were many more machines per voter in many suburban areas than in urban areas. The *Washington Post* reported that in the county including Columbus, "27 of the 30 wards with the most machines per registered voter showed majorities for Bush. At the other end of the spectrum, six of the seven wards with the fewest machines delivered large margins for Kerry."[41] The *Post* estimates up to 15,000 lost votes in Columbus alone. Secretary of State Blackwell resisted a judge's order to make backup provisional ballots more widely available, comparing himself to Mohandas Gandhi, Martin Luther King, and the apostle Paul, all of whom went to jail.[42] Eventually he prevailed in court. An investigation by the minority staff of the House Judiciary Committee found that in just one polling place, Blackwell's stance cost more than 1,100 votes.[43] Ohio spewed a blizzard of bizarre rules designed to make it harder for private groups to stage voter registration drives. They evoked the scene in Woody

Allen's movie *Bananas*, where the caudillo issues a stream of increasingly absurd commands. ("All citizens will be required to change their underwear every half hour. Underwear will be worn on the outside so we can check.") The edicts included rejecting voter registration forms that were not printed on 80-pound paper, requiring paid voter registration workers to take an online course run by Blackwell's office, and threatening registration drive organizers with criminal penalties if the forms were not returned directly to his office. That last measure was struck down by a federal court.[44]

Ohio exemplified the worst, but we came achingly close to a massive crack-up all over the country on Election Day 2006. The recent federal voter law ordered states to pull together county voter lists and create a statewide computerized database. States are supposed to double-check information on the registration forms as a safeguard. Early in 2006, the Brennan Center looked into how states were doing the clerical work. Many states simply checked the voter records against another list, say, the driver's license registry. But in some states, if bureaucrats found any variation in the data, the voter was kept off the rolls. On Election Day, a perfectly eligible voter, who had never heard of any trouble, would show up at the polling place and discover that her name was mysteriously missing. The euphemism for this system of confirming voter lists is "no match, no vote." More accurately, it's disenfranchisement-by-typo.

Such goofs are surprisingly common. A trial run of the system in New York City showed that one-fifth of eligible registrants could have been barred from voting due to errors. Women often change their names when they marry. An official could accidentally type "Locke" instead of "Lock" or "Reid" instead of "Reed." The federal government checked, and learned it could find a Social Security match for voter information only half the time. Ethnic or foreign-sounding names often are simply misunderstood or misspelled by registrars. Think of the great basketball player Yao Ming, all seven feet six of him. Yao is actually his surname—Ming is his first name. If you didn't know that, voter registrars might not either.

All told, the Brennan Center had every reason to expect that hundreds of thousands of voters would face a surprise disenfranchisement on Election Day. In the spring of 2006, the center released a report showing which states were the worst.[45] Within days, some state officials called us, and worked to fix their lists. Some wouldn't budge. In May 2006, we went to federal court in Washington State, representing the Washington Association of Churches, Asian American associations, the Service Employees International Union, and the antipoverty group ACORN. The groups sued to stop "no match, no vote." The situation was ideal, not only because Washington had a bad system, but also because the practice was backed up by a state statute, thus far easier to challenge in court than an off-the-books practice. A win there would ripple throughout the country.

Washington State argued, in effect, that it did not make mistakes, or if it did, it corrected them. The state, its lawyers assured the court, was very, very careful. There was one problem for Washington's argument: *The front page of the state's brief defending the law, in which it made this argument, misspelled the name of the judge.*

Persuaded, one presumes, by more than by the misspelling of his name, Judge Ricardo Martinez froze the implementation of the law. It is "clear," he ruled, "that federal law was intended to put in place administrative safeguards for "storing and managing the official list of registered voters," and not to add a restriction on voter eligibility.[46] By Election Day 2006, all but a handful of states had met the challenge. Hundreds of thousands of voters never knew that they had narrowly missed being blocked from the rolls, a fact they otherwise would have discovered the hard way: on Election Day.

Political Purges: Manipulating the Voter Lists

Once voters are on the registration rolls, there is no guarantee they will not be purged (that is, kicked off). Here we have not just *silent* disenfranchisement, but *secret* disenfranchisement. And because voter lists are now statewide and computerized, voters can more easily be struck from the rolls with the click of a mouse.

Officials naturally seek to weed the rolls. Voters move and die. Lists have errors and duplications. But local administrators routinely conduct legally required purges with no publicly known standards and no accountability. Purges rarely are publicly announced. Often, states do not notify voters when their names are removed. Such purges without oversight or standards can be subject to political manipulation that would seem charmingly familiar to Boss Tweed and his confederates.

Unsurprisingly, the dragnet sweeps up many citizens who are in fact eligible. In 2000, Florida hired a private company to scrub the voter rolls. In all, 58,000 voters were targeted for removal. One news investigation found that at least 15 percent of names were included by error.[47] Half of the purged voters in Dade County who appealed their removal were deemed to actually be eligible, but by then it was too late.[48] Among those wrongly purged was Wallace McDonald, who was never convicted of any felony, but had once committed the misdemeanor of falling asleep on a park bench, and thus was added to the list.[49] Although a few Florida counties diligently investigated the names passed along by the state, many simply got the list and made the purge without asking questions. The private company's spokesman gamely defended the high error rate to the online magazine *Salon* as a "minor glitch," adding ruefully, "I guess that's a little bit embarrassing in light of the election."[50] Of course, given the state's 537-vote margin that decided the presidency, that "glitch" looked like a landslide.

Secret purges are ripe for partisan mischief. In 2004, Florida planned to purge another 48,000 "suspected felons" from the voting rolls. But the list contained the names of 22,000 African Americans, and only 63 Hispanics. (That's not a misprint.) Of note, Florida is the one state in the country where blacks and Hispanics vote for different political parties:

blacks largely for the Democrats, while Hispanics, heavily Cuban, traditionally tilt Republican. (Such coincidences are certainly marvelous.) In any event, under pressure from voting rights groups, Florida ordered officials to stop using the purge list statewide. Even so, some counties apparently used the same discredited, discontinued list to purge the rolls before Election Day anyway.[51]

The Push for Voter ID

In recent years, a fierce drive has sought to enact strict, new voter ID laws. These statutes would require an otherwise eligible citizen to produce a government ID in order to be able to vote on Election Day. The U.S. House of Representatives voted to require proffering proof of citizenship to cast a ballot. Indiana and Georgia demand a government-issued photo ID card. Other states are readying similar measures, waiting for the courts to give a sign of encouragement.

It is easy to understand the appeal of voter ID laws. After all, voters must be who they say they are. Nobody wants fraud (or at least nobody should). The dead should rest in peace, not be a voting bloc. But the idea of massive "voter fraud" is itself a fraud. The truth about "voter fraud" is that, by and large, it doesn't exist.

Of course, the United States boasts a long tradition of *election* fraud—shenanigans orchestrated by political parties and corrupt machines. Governor Earl Long once quipped, "When I die—if I die—I want to be buried in Louisiana, so

I can stay active in politics."[52] Robert Caro memorably recounts how "Landslide Lyndon" Johnson won his first Senate race by 87 votes only after his partisans discovered a previously overlooked ballot box filled with 203 ballots.[53] John F. Kennedy openly joked about rumors the Chicago Democratic machine stole the 1960 election. "They said terrible things about you, but I never believed it," he told a group of precinct workers, before asking them to do it again for the local slate.[54] Such stories are the lore of American politics. While open boss-led jiggering of vote totals appears to be largely a thing of the past, there is still a risk of the manipulation of electronic voting machines and absentee ballots, both of which require coordinated insider effort.

But voter fraud by *individuals* is rare indeed, and simple logic shows why. At the risk of five years in federal prison, a $10,000 fine, and, indeed, of having the right to vote taken away, someone would have to *really* support a candidate to illegally cast even one extra vote.[55] Undocumented immigrants, often scapegoated, are even less likely to illegally vote en masse. We can hardly expect a recent illegal arrival from Mexico to cross the border, evade capture ... and then stroll into a government office and give her name and address! The Secretary of State of Georgia confirmed that she had never encountered a single case of voter impersonation.[56] During the Justice Department's five-year nationwide push to prosecute voter fraud, through several elections, exactly eighty-six people were convicted in a country of 300 million—and none for any crime that voter ID would stop.

An individual is more likely to be struck and killed by lightning than to commit voter fraud.

Upon investigation, lurid allegations usually turn out to reveal simple mistakes by voters or poll workers.[57] Typical was Ali Usman, a sixty-eight-year-old jewelry store owner from Miami and a legal resident of the United States, who hurriedly filled out a voter registration form a clerk handed him at the Department of Motor Vehicles. He never voted. With his daughter and wife, both American citizens, Usman was deported to Pakistan for improperly filling out the voter card. "We're foreigners here," he lamented to *The New York Times.*[58] In St. Louis in 2001, partisans announced grimly that seventy-nine voters had registered as living in vacant lots. The *St. Louis Post Dispatch* investigated and found that nearly all had homes on the property—the city records were wrong.[59] Then there was a list of supposedly dead voters in upstate New York much touted in October 2006. When reporters looked into names on the list, it turned out that the voters were, to paraphrase Monty Python, "not dead yet."[60]

In any case, for those still worried about voter impersonation, the law already has ways to require people to verify their identity. Consider the Help America Vote Act. Under that law, if someone registers by mail, they can either provide a Social Security number or show some proof of identity at the polls. But the proof isn't tightly limited. The voter can show a government-issued photo ID, such as a driver's license or a veteran's card, or some other proof such as a utility bill, a paycheck or government check, or any other government document that shows where the voter currently lives. Few Americans lack every single one of these pieces of paperwork. Even simpler and more widely used is the simple method of checking a voter's signature against a photocopy on the registration form. Unless you are a forger, it is surprisingly hard to precisely match the penmanship. This method is used millions of times every year without opening the way to fraud.

In short, if the goal of requiring ID to vote is truly to prove who everyone is, that is conceptually possible and relatively easy. But the new ID laws are carefully crafted not to require IDs that people do have, but the ones that many simply *don't* have. It is hard for middle-class Americans to realize that many of our fellow citizens don't have the ID we take for granted.

All told, one in ten Americans simply doesn't have a government-issued photo ID—twenty million voters or more.[61] There are 196 million licensed drivers, but 227 million voting-age citizens. Some are simply too poor to own a car, and thus have no reason to wait in line and get a license.[62] Others live in cities such as New York, where residents are more likely to wield a subway Metrocard than a stick shift. In Wisconsin, for example, very few college students have a photo ID with a current address (dorms don't count), and one quarter of elderly Wisconsin residents lack a driver's license or photo ID.[63]

Even more worrisome are proposals that voters produce documents to prove citizenship. Most Americans lack a passport, since they have never traveled outside the country. As for birth certificates, some admirably organized individuals have their original; the rest of us have to arrange to get a copy from the county in which we were born. These various proof-of-citizenship documents can cost from $40 (for a passport) up to $200 (for proof of naturalization, say, for an immigrant who came to the country decades ago). By contrast, the infamous poll tax, when it was deemed unconstitutional in 1966, was worth $8.97 in today's dollars. Again, all this paperwork is needed only to prove citizenship so one can vote. When voting rights backers call ID requirements a "new poll tax," it's not rhetoric—it's math.

There's much evidence that the worst forms of voter ID would, in fact, turn away real people. Political scientists from three universities queried voters as they left polling places in 2006. They found that many voters would not have had the necessary ID had strict laws been in place—and minority and immigrant voters were the least likely to have the needed paperwork. The political scientists concluded that a strict ID policy, if in place, could have changed the outcome of a dozen or more House races in 2006.[64] Such concerns seem beside the point to some. A confidential Justice Department memo paraphrases an interview with the Georgia law's chief sponsor, Rep. Sue Burmeister, who suggested that "if there are fewer black voters because of this bill, it will only be because there is less opportunity for fraud."[65]

It all amounts to a political perpetual motion machine. As elections approach, vaporous stories of widespread fraud are pumped into the air. The very fear of imaginary fraud then triggers policies that block real voters from the polls. Right before the 2006 election, Arizona passed a law imposing an onerous new ID requirement. A judge froze the law, granting a preliminary injunction sought by civil rights advocates on the grounds that the remedy would prevent many legitimate voters from casting ballots. The case rushed up to the U.S. Supreme Court. In an unsigned opinion, the Court unfroze the ID law and let it go forward on technical grounds. But the anonymous justice who wrote for the Court also set out reasoning ("dicta") that drew a roadmap for disenfranchisement. True, the ID rules might disenfranchise real voters, the justice wrote. But the anxiety about fraud itself creates a kind of disenfranchisement too. "Voter fraud drives honest citizens out of the democratic process and breeds distrust of our government," the unnamed Supreme Court justice wrote. "Voters who *fear* their legitimate votes will be outweighed by fraudulent ones will *feel disenfranchised*" (emphasis added).[66] Historian Alex Keyssar mocked, "FEEL disenfranchised? Is that the same as 'being disenfranchised'? So if I might 'feel' disenfranchised, I have a right to make it harder for you to vote?"[67]

Others were more open about the blunt political logic. Royal Masset, the former political director of the Texas Republican Party, was unnervingly candid in an interview with the *Houston Chronicle,* as reported in May 2007.

> *Among Republicans, [the Chronicle reported] it is an "article of religious faith that voter fraud is causing us to lose elections," Masset said. He doesn't agree with that, but*

does believe that requiring photo IDs could cause enough of a dropoff in legitimate Democratic voting to add 3 percent to the Republican vote.[68]

It is well past time to stop treating voting as an artifact of partisan combat. A great democracy does not properly see the administering of elections as proper terrain for underhanded conduct. The next step in modernizing our elections is to create new national approaches that improve voting, block disenfranchising moves, and boost turnout by making it easy to vote.

CREATE A NEW NATIONAL VOTER REGISTRATION STANDARD

We are one country. Americans don't tolerate regional differences in the number of espresso shots in a Starbucks Americano or the number of pickle slices on a Big Mac, yet we accept them when it comes to voting.

As the Supreme Court ruled in *Bush v. Gore,* it is wrong and probably unconstitutional for votes to be counted differently in one place than in another. Senator Hillary Clinton and Rep. Stephanie Tubbs Jones have proposed the "Count Every Vote Act."[69] It is as close as any bill has come to a "gold standard" for voter registration and election administration. Just as a Voting Rights Act was necessary to overrule southern states' tendencies to autocratic rule, this proposed law would create a federal floor—a uniform minimum standard—to protect eligible voters from bad registration practices as they crop up around the country. "Count Every Vote" would do several key things.

- It would boost nonpartisan and professional election administration, by instituting training of poll workers and letting nonpartisan observers have greater access to the polls.
- It would push states to offer the best practices, ranging from ending permanent felony disenfranchisement to Election Day registration.
- It would set national standards for how many voting machines should be in place per thousand voters. That is a good way to avoid the problem, seen in Ohio in 2004 and elsewhere, of long lines snaking outside polling places in poor neighborhoods, while suburban voters breeze through without a lengthy wait.

ELECTION DAY, EVERY DAY

Once we make it possible for people to register and vote, we need to get them to actually do it—and that means clearing away all the remaining barriers to participation.

There are at least two strong reasons we should care about low voter turnout. The first, simply, is that government can't represent the full spectrum of public views if the full electorate doesn't participate. If poorer people and less educated people feel cut off, their interests will be represented less well. And not surprisingly, those are the people less likely to make it to the polls to vote. More than that, voting is an essential element of citizenship. We should not view it as a privilege, yet it is not enough to view it as a right—we should view it as a duty, a part of everyone's obligation to participate. So we should make it as convenient as possible for people to fulfill that duty.

Creative ideas abound. Jonathan Soros has proposed a highly innovative national presidential primary with voting from January to June, with tallies announced every month. That way, citizens who aren't in Iowa or New Hampshire would get equal say in picking nominees, with voter interest piqued by the drama.[70] Australia and Belgium, for their part, actually require citizens to go to the polls.[71] Citizens must pay taxes and serve on juries; voting is just as important. Such a measure would boost participation and actually is a very sound idea in principle, but it is sharply unpopular and runs too hard against our libertarian grain. (Remember, Australia began as penal colony!) Goofier ideas abound, too. A referendum on the ballot in Arizona in 2006 would have given a lottery ticket potentially worth $1 million to everyone who votes. It was rejected overwhelmingly by currently uncompensated voters.[72]

Some argue that we simply ought not aim for more voting. If people can't be bothered to care enough about issues or elections to show up, why is that bad? They echo those at the Constitutional Convention who warned that a wide franchise would mean government by the ignorant. But many nonvoters do want to cast ballots—it is simply that the current system makes Election Day cumbersome or hard to vote on. So why not make it easier for those who do want to vote? Let's explore some ways to do that.

We assume that "the first Tuesday after the first Monday in November" is sacrosanct, perhaps written into the Constitution. Actually, it's a law passed by Congress in 1845—to make it possible for a nation of farmers to vote. As journalist David Broder recently explained, the harvest is over by November (but winter hasn't set in). Saturday was a work day, and Sunday was the Sabbath. To get to the county seat, where voting was held, often was a day's carriage ride. And Wednesday was market day. Hence, Tuesday.[73] This is quaint and charming, but not a great reason to stick with a day that depresses turnout. Today, voting on a Tuesday means people have to miss work, arrive late or leave early, only to brave long lines (and possibly turn away in frustration). Many lack child care. Elderly or infirm voters can't easily get to the polls. According to the U.S. Census Bureau, the main reason people give for not being able to vote is scheduling conflicts and business responsibilities.[74]

One often-proposed solution would be to make Election Day a federal holiday. What better way to fuse patriotism with the core patriotic act of choosing our leaders? But just as with Veteran's Day or Labor Day, the original purpose of many federal holidays tends to fade into an opportunity to shop or barbecue. Election Day as a holiday may do some good, since more public buildings would be available as polling places, and some people would get the day off. But other problems might worsen. After all, many people still have to work on holidays, especially lower-wage workers at retail stores and restaurants and in service jobs—thus keeping them from voting and driving up overtime costs for businesses. A better idea might be to hold elections over two days—such as over a weekend. (That way neither Christians nor Jews would have to stay home for religious reasons.) Logically, two days would make it easier for voters to get to the polls one way or another, and would give campaigns more time to contact supporters.

In Oregon, there are no long lines or buggy voting machines at local polling places—because there are no polling places. It's the one state in the nation where all voting is now done by mail. Everyone is mailed a ballot, which they must mail back or bring to a county drop-box. The system is popular in Oregon. Boosters argue it spurs turnout, while making it easier to count votes since they come in over a period of weeks rather than all in one chaotic day. This is part of a nationwide trend to allow voters to cast ballots before Election Day. Thirty-one states allow in-person early voting.[75] In Arizona, half the ballots are cast before Election Day.[76]

Still, Oregon stands out for eliminating Election Day altogether. Is it a good idea? The move does not seem to have hurt turnout, but it hasn't helped much, either. Oregon was sixth in the nation before vote-by-mail, and is sixth in the nation now (at a lower rate).[77] There are some significant problems with an entirely vote-by-mail system. In part, the approach is only as good as the U.S. Postal Service. Ballots mailed to voters often are wrongly returned to sender, "addressee unknown." Absentee or mail voting also poses a greater risk of fraud, or of people being coerced to vote for one candidate or another (say, while an employer watches). Many people regret the loss of the civic ritual that comes from showing up at a polling place. Beyond sentimentality, it is simply harder (and sometimes more expensive) for campaigns to reach disparate individual voters to turn them out to vote. A better fix is to allow "no excuses absentee voting." Most voting is done in person. But if a citizen wants to cast an absentee ballot, she or he can do so without having to claim illness or a business trip, as is the case today. The Count Every Vote Act would require states to allow it. Not a bad thing—if it is combined with other steps to boost turnout and improve accuracy on Election Day itself.

Assuming we make it so that all citizens are registered, and obstacles to their voting are cleared away, we will need to address the third major barrier to public confidence in elections: the risk of error or fraud in the new system of electronic voting machines.

3

STOP POLITICAL "HACKING"

Rewiring Electronic Voting

In 2006, the race in Florida's Thirteenth Congressional district was excruciatingly close, and Republican Vern Buchanan won by 369 votes. But something very odd happened with the vote count in the biggest county in the district, the communities where Democratic candidate Christine Jennings ran strongest. In that one county, 18 percent of the voters who went to the polls were recorded as not voting at all in the pivotal congressional race.[78] This mysterious drop-off happened only on one brand of voting machine. By contrast, only 2 or 3 percent of those voting on other machines or by absentee ballot were recorded as skipping the congressional race. A Dartmouth professor testifying on behalf of the manufacturer asserted that voters misread the confusing ballot on the electronic screen. But he admitted in court that whatever the reason, these undervotes probably tipped the election.[79]

This was just the most glaring glitch yet in the introduction of electronic voting systems. In 2008, nearly all voters in every state but New York will have their votes tallied by electronic machines. Many Americans fret their votes won't count—and it turns out they have very good reason to worry.

Before 2000, few communities used electronic systems. The Florida debacle underscored how dilapidated machines could turn a vote count into a farce. The Votomatic machines used in Florida were once state of the art, for a time when punch cards were as magical as an iPhone is today. After the debacle that taught us the difference between "hanging chads" and "pregnant chads," electronic machines were pushed as a panacea. In a fervor reminiscent of the Internet bubble, lobbyists for voting machine companies insisted that the new machines would count accurately and be impervious to error. The Help America Vote Act passed by Congress essentially required states to switch to electronic machines.

Today, counties use two types of electronic systems. In "direct recording electric," or DRE, machines, voters register a choice by tapping a touchscreen. (Think of a Treo or an ATM.) Many of these touchscreen machines have no paper record at all. With Optical Scan machines, a voter marks a ballot by hand and the machine reads it. (Think of a fill-in-the-bubble standardized test, such as the SATs.)

Almost immediately, many voters began to worry that touchscreens, in particular, were insecure, that they could be programmed to tilt results one way or another. Many Democrats were alarmed when the CEO of voting machine manufacturer Diebold pledged he was "committed to helping Ohio deliver its electoral votes to the president next year."[80] *Rolling Stone* published an article asserting that the difference between exit polls and the final result suggested that the will of Ohio voters had been "subverted."[81] In fact, for all the worries, there was little evidence that tampering with machines changed the Ohio result. (It is true that there weren't enough machines in inner-city neighborhoods, and that failure of machines in Democratic polling places led to long lines and likely resulted in the loss of thousands of votes. But that's different from the machines themselves sneakily voting "Bush" when the voter tapped "Kerry.") But the concerns were widespread and serious enough to deserve a full airing. It seemed that some actual facts might be in order.

The Brennan Center convened many of the nation's top computer scientists and election protection experts in a Task Force on Voting System Security. Its members came from inside the federal government, private business, and universities such as MIT and Stanford. The panel included Howard Schmidt, former chief security officer of Microsoft who later served as President George W. Bush's cybersecurity czar. The experts sorted out all the various ways a hacker could attack the machines. Then they reviewed security measures that the manufacturers or government officials had put in place to protect them.

After nearly two years of study, the Task Force concluded alarmingly and unanimously: *Every single electronic voting system used in the United States is dangerously hackable.*

When it comes to voting, as the old saying goes, "even paranoids have enemies."

The Task Force pointed to several risks. It would be possible to insert hard-to-detect "malicious software" into machines that would mysteriously shift votes from one candidate to another. A bug that moved just one vote per machine could add enough votes to a candidate's total to tip a close election. The scientists pointed to the case of Ron Harris, a computer technician for Nevada's Gaming Control Board. He hid a software attack program in dozens of video-poker and slot machines in the early 1990s. A pal could trigger jackpots by placing bets in a specific order. "Mr. Harris was eventually caught because he became too brazen: by the mid-1990s, he began using an attack program against the gaming machines based on the card game 'Keno.' When his accomplice attempted to redeem a $100,000 jackpot, officials became suspicious and she was ultimately investigated and caught."[82] According to the Task Force, such malicious codes could too easily be slipped into election systems, too. Most alarming, in every state but Minnesota and New York, machines are allowed to have wireless components. A hacker with a modicum of savvy and a Blackberry could stroll into a polling station and steal an election by triggering a software attack. As the Task Force reported, "Few jurisdictions have implemented any of the key countermeasures that could make the least difficult attacks against voting systems much more difficult to execute successfully."

Others confirmed the study's findings. Just a few months after the Brennan Center report was released, a team of scientists from Princeton University appeared before Congress to demonstrate one of the attacks on a commonly used touchscreen machine. In December 2006, the National Institute of Standards and Technology, the federal government's expert think tank, concluded that paperless systems "cannot be made secure."[83] In 2007, California's new Secretary of State Deborah Bowen convened her own expert task force. It found that computer company insiders or election officials could tamper with the systems then in use in Los Angeles and elsewhere.

Some argue that the threat from electronic voting is overblown. After all, we have no firm evidence of any elections being stolen this way, despite all worries. But such calm is unwarranted. After all, politicians have been stuffing ballot boxes since senators wore togas. There's simply no reason to think they would stop now. Technology has changed, but human nature hasn't.

Beyond fraud, we do know that the machines are dismayingly prone to misvotes, freezing up, and other errors familiar to any owner of a balky home computer. In 2006, we saw dozens of examples, including programming errors, failing machines, and software bugs in over thirty states that lost or mistallied tens of thousands of votes. Even assuming we lived in a world without corruption, we certainly do not live in a world without mistakes. These flaws in security are also flaws in reliability. They will lead to massive numbers of lost votes, unless basic countermeasures are taken.

In fact, such elemental steps can make a huge difference. The Task Force found several remedies that could make electronic voting more secure and reliable.

Why Not Just Junk the Machines?

Many grassroots citizen activists who had the most to do with blowing the whistle on electronic voting want to take this step. They view other possible remedies as incomplete, overly complex, and prone to the same problems seen today. Brad Friedman, whose blog is a widely read electronic bulletin board on electronic voting issues, writes, "The fact is: There is no way to verify that a voter's vote is correctly *cast* on a DRE touch-screen voting machine. Period."[84]

Still, it wouldn't make sense to pass a law banning the electronic machines, for a few reasons. For starters, the good old days before electronic voting weren't so great. Experts routinely calculated that 2 to 3 percent of all votes in earlier elections were miscounted. The Caltech/MIT Voting Technology Project estimated that in the 2000 election, before states were required to purchase electronic machines, "between 4 and 6 million votes were lost due to problems with voting machines, voter registration and polling place practices."[85] MIT professor Charles Stewart concluded that lost votes are down significantly since then, especially because the new machines don't let voters accidentally pick two candidates.[86] He concluded that as many as one million new votes may now have been properly recorded.

The second reason we can't simply junk the machines is cost. We're not starting from nothing. Almost every county outside of New York State now has purchased new electronic machines. It would be caprice to simply discard those expenditures, and start over, especially if adequate fixes are available.

There's a third reason to try to fix the electronic systems, if possible. For some Americans, well-run electronic machines can work better than the old lever machines or punch-card ballots. Think of the notorious "butterfly ballot" in Palm Beach County, Florida, in 2000, which led thousands of elderly Jews to accidentally vote for anti-Israel candidate Pat Buchanan when they meant to vote for Al Gore. (*Oy gevalt!*) Or think of the hundreds of voters in northern Florida who checked off Al Gore and then for good measure wrote his name in too, thus invalidating their ballot under a mindless rule. In fact, advocates for people with disabilities have argued that touchscreen machines are the best way to empower millions who could not previously vote without giving up privacy and dignity, especially the blind. It is also much easier to give a voter a ballot in Spanish, Russian, or Chinese using an electronic machine than to print up dozens of foreign-language documents. We should not simply cast aside these concerns as frivolous.

USE TREE-BASED TECHNOLOGY

In fact, there are specific ways to fix the electronic machines so they are more secure and make fewer errors. The first and by far most important fix could use an innovative, flexible technology derived from tree products: paper.[87] Every voter should get a piece of paper that he or she can use to make sure that the machine is recording the correct preference. It would also create a record that can be checked against the final total to look for error or fraud. If need be, the paper can serve as the basis for a recount. The "Optical Scan" systems use paper already, since that's how voters mark their ballots. In some instances it is also possible to hook up a printer to the touchscreen machines to produce a record.

Experts agree that touchscreen machines *without* a paper record are dangerously insecure. At a dramatic midnight press conference on July 2007, just minutes before a six-month legal deadline expired, California's voting chief Deborah Bowen announced she would decertify nearly all the voting machines in the state. She then recertified only those with paper records. As a practical matter, this discarded the touch-screen machines then in use through much of the state.

REMEMBER THE HUMAN ELEMENT

The Brennan Center report found something else, some-thing a bit more surprising. It turns out that even paper isn't worth much without the human element. Election officials must conduct surprise, random audits on Election Day or soon after, to match the paper records with the machine total. Otherwise, the piles of paper make voters feel better but don't help find errors. Twelve states conduct such "post-election" audits. They found that the audits can be done quickly and without much cost. Unfortunately, the rest still have not required this basic measure.

And pollworkers who run these systems need training. Local officials can be forgiven for being frustrated and confused. Federal law ordered them to buy new machines; they were then stampeded into buying expensive touch-screen devices. Now they are being told the systems they just purchased are insecure. When a message appears on a home computer from Microsoft warning of a security risk, most people just click on the "fix it" button (without knowing what they've just done). These local officials are being told, in effect, "You have a security risk. You fix it." Pollworkers are often public spirited but elderly, called into service once or twice every two years for the sense of doing good. But an entirely new system of electronic machines needs a more professionalized squad to run them. Just before the 2006 primaries Maryland advertised for "technical workers" on the website Monster.com. These hired-off-the-street "experts" got a few hours training, then were deployed throughout the state. The potential for political election chicanery ranks only with the potential for incompetence.

Voters need to be trained, too. The first time many of us used an ATM or a PC, we probably made some mistakes. We used those devices frequently enough that we were able to learn the way they work. But people who err in the first two or three times they vote on a DRE have just been disenfranchised. Many polling places lack posted instruc-tions, or better yet, a sample machine to learn on (and voters almost never get a sample ballot that looks like the screen they will actually vote on).

FEDERAL REFORM AND LOCAL ACTION

In the year and a half since the Brennan Center report, a solid consensus has formed that electronic voting—without paper records, audits, and other basic security measures—poses an unacceptable risk. Yet few states have put in place the changes needed to make voting secure, reliable, and accurate.

As of September 2007, voters in twelve states still used touchscreen machines without a paper record—the single system most vulnerable to security risks. More significant, most states do not routinely perform audits. Even where there are paper records, only thirteen states require audits of those paper records in all their counties. And no state— not one—has adopted procedures to catch the most clever software-based attacks.[88]

Plainly, federal action to set some minimum and uniform standards makes sense. The Brennan Center testified before the Senate Rules Committee in February of 2007 on the voting machines, the first hearing of the new Congress on any voting issue. The session offered a microcosm of the difficulty of making change. Senators wandered in and out, whispering to aides and paying fitful attention. At one point, as Rep. Rush Holt, an actual nuclear physicist, testified alongside former astronaut Sen. Bill Nelson, a colleague glibly assured them the issue was "not rocket science." During testimony warning that electronic voting systems had wireless components, the committee chair interrupted earnestly, asking, "What is a 'wireless component'?" One solon sat silently through the testimony, then averred that he thought all this voter machine talk was fine, but the real trouble came from voter fraud and needed to be cured by restrictive IDs. The hearing ended in a colloquy over whether LBJ would have had an easier time stuffing the ballot boxes in Texas if the machines had been electronic. Ill omens abounded.

Despite the difficulties, a federal law still makes sense. The best bill for the past several years was introduced by Rep. Holt, a New Jersey Democrat, and Rep. Tom Davis, a Virginia Republican. They won support from a majority of House members throughout 2007. But quick action stalled, as so often happens in Washington. Local officials moaned that Washington was imposing yet another "unfunded mandate," ordering states to solve a problem without providing financial help to do it. At the same time, advocates for foreign-language-speaking communities and the disabled weighed in. They were fearful that what they saw as real progress could be swept away in a panicked rush to discard the electronic systems. Democratic congressional leaders convened reformers and disability advocates for months of tendentious talks. The legislation ground to a halt.

To have an impact for the 2008 elections, states will have to step in—and many have. Florida Governor Charlie Crist stood with Democratic congressman Robert Wexler to announce legislation requiring a voter-verified paper record and an audit. California made much the same call, in the wake of the decertification orchestrated by Secretary of State Bowen.

Whether the fixes are made by Washington or in state capitals, it can't be done without more money. We spend five billion dollars *a month* to spread democracy to Iraq—but we have spent less than that in the full *six years* since the Florida electoral debacle to entirely update our voting systems. The nation has changed the way it casts and counts votes with unprecedented speed. It would be unreasonable to believe this could happen without adequate funding. The Help America Vote Act set aside about $3 billion (over five years) to help states buy the new machines and set up state voter databases. But states didn't even draw on all the money, leaving much of it unspent. Complex voting security systems, in thousands of jurisdictions, involving tens of thousands of laypeople, cannot properly be created in short order without a substantial new infusion of funds.

Citizens often look at their ATMs, and note that those electronic machines seem fully able to register their touch. They note that ATMs do not give them the wrong amount. "And certainly it has never given me too much money!" The fact is that banks spend considerably more in a year for upkeep and repair on their ATM systems than our nation has spent over six years to entirely modernize its voting technology.[89] In this instance, we got what we paid for.

★ ★ ★

By tearing down barriers to participation and finally engaging the government in the task of encouraging participation, we will take the first key step toward renewing our system. A massive influx of new voters will change the complexion of policymaking. It will connect millions more Americans more directly to the civic act of choosing leaders, as well. But fixing our voting system will not, in itself, restore a working democracy. There are too many huge obstacles: ways in which the system tilts toward organized and wealthy interests, and ways in which the rules dampen competition. We now turn to those challenges.

REFORMING POLITICS

PART TWO: REFORMING POLITICS

L et's assume, for the moment, that we fix our voting system. Whom will people be thrilled to vote *for?* We can sigh about the quality of candidates, pine for another Abraham Lincoln or Teddy Roosevelt, or obsess about the character quirks and personal foibles of politicians. But we won't get better politicians until we get better politics. And just as in the area of voting, while many basic institutions of American politics are broken, they can be fixed.

The United States is the only Western democracy where it's illegal to limit campaign spending, where candidates must pay tens of millions of dollars to speak to voters on TV, where legislators routinely draw and redraw the lines of their own electoral districts, where the person who comes in second in a two-person race can still be made president. When we proudly talk about American exceptionalism, this isn't what we have in mind.

All these serve to limit the choices given to voters. At too many levels of government, incumbent reelection rates in the United States rival the Supreme Soviet (in the Brezhnev era, no less!). Incumbents overwhelmingly outspend their challengers. And when it comes to presidential elections, for the one person charged with representing all the people, most voters never see an active campaign, because they live in a state that is reliably "red" or "blue." For most Americans, a presidential campaign is something they hear about—it happens far away.

We cannot ignite a democracy movement unless we address the way laws keep competition at bay. Even universal voter registration will become a vehicle for mass disillusionment if we don't fix politics, too. After all, Saddam Hussein's final election had 100 percent turnout, and he won 100 percent of the vote.[90] People need something real to vote for. Fortunately, concrete reforms in the way we pay for and run campaigns can markedly improve voter choice, and voluntary public funding of elections would free up candidates to seek the vote and meet the concerns of millions more ordinary citizens. And an end to partisan gerrymandering and the Electoral College will at last give more voters more of a voice in more campaigns than ever before.

4

CAMPAIGN FINANCE REFORM

Public Financing, an Old Idea Whose Time Has Come

Our campaign finance system is arguably the worst in the Western world. It is, of course, often garishly corrupt. It is also deeply absurd. Many candidates spend *most* of their time raising funds, overwhelmingly from private interests seeking to sway legislation, only to fork over the bulk of the money they collect to television broadcasters for access to the airwaves provided free in every other major democracy (where allowed at all). A combination of tangled laws, technology, and greed has conspired to create a system that elevates donors over voters.

It's hardly news that wealthy interests hold special sway in politics. As one-time speaker of the California legislature Jesse Unruh memorably said, "Money is the mother's milk of politics." For as long as money has crowded in on politics, reformers have tried to push it back. There has been a cycle of corruption and reform throughout history. This was true even before today's campaign finance system. In the nineteenth century, campaigns were paid for by patronage appointees who worked for the government. Everyone knew it was wrong. But only after President James A. Garfield was assassinated by a spurned job-seeker in 1881 did Congress finally pass the first campaign finance and civil service reforms that put up a wall between government workers and attempts to raise money for political candidates.

Then in the Gilded Age of the late 1800s, when massive new industrial corporations began to dominate the market-place, government often appeared little more than an appendage of economic power. Pennsylvania famously was so controlled by John D. Rockefeller, one wag said, that Standard Oil had done everything to the legislature but refine it. In 1896, Mark Hannah created the model for modern campaign fundraising by dunning corporations for contributions to support William McKinley's GOP presi-dential campaign against the threat of populist candidate William Jennings Bryan. As America's business culture became nationalized, so did campaign finance.

The new system of private campaign finance tainted even President Theodore Roosevelt. After it was revealed that TR had received large donations from the insurance industry in 1904, he felt his honor had been besmirched. "Sooner or later, unless there is a readjustment, there will come a riotous, wicked, murderous day of atonement," he told a reporter, and eventually he won passage of the first federal law banning campaign contributions from corporations.[91]

Such private power advances and recedes in cycles. During periods of reform, laws change and institutions are created that reassert the ability of democracy to function without being fully dominated by organized money. During other periods, private business broadens its reach. Yes, it is tempting to look at the role of money in politics today and sigh, "Unappealing, of course. But that's the way it always has been." But it is important to understand just how much things have changed in recent decades.

Campaign giving and spending have exploded. From 1976 to 2004, living costs tripled, but congressional campaign costs rose *tenfold*.[92] Overwhelmingly, these funds flow to incumbents, protecting them from competition with strong challengers. Even in 2006, when surging Democrats swept into office across the country, winning challengers on average spent barely half of what the incumbents spent.[93] Year in and year out, about 95 percent of House winners outspend their opponents.[94] As Will Rogers said in a far more innocent time, "Politics has got so expensive that it takes lots of money to even get beat with."

Increasingly, legislatures are as moneyed as the ski slopes at Aspen. Robert F. Kennedy warned, "We are in danger of creating a situation in which our candidates must be chosen from among the rich [like the Kennedys themselves] . . . or those willing to be beholden to others."[95] Kennedy's dystopia is today's mundane reality. In one recent calculus, as of 2002 a greater share of greatly wealthy individuals were serving in the senate than was the case in 1912, when the number was so high it helped prompt a constitutional amendment giving citizens the right to vote for senators, instead of corrupt state legislatures.[96] (In the polite euphemism, these are "self-financing" candidates.)

The cash chase warps politics in other, less visible ways. For candidates, the one irreducible task is not meeting voters or crafting positions, but raising funds. Mark Green, the former New York City public advocate, calls it a "time thief." After thousands of phone calls and visits to potential donors, he wrote, "It's hard to overstate the physical and psychological stamina required in such an effort, and how little time and energy it leaves for all else."[97] Former Senator Alan Simpson of Wyoming, once the Republican Whip, bemoaned, "Incumbents find it eternally necessary to raise big bucks for their next election nearly every single day. It's not only demeaning but it took a large chunk of time that could have been devoted to doing the public's business."[98] Lawmakers routinely can be found at the congressional campaign committees near the Capitol, dialing prospective donors, pulled away from their day job of legislating. The scene resembles less *Mr. Smith Goes to Washington* and more *Glengarry, Glen Ross.*

When political professionals scout a possible office-holder, the first question they ask is, "Is he a credible candidate?"—which refers not to whether he tells the truth but to his ability to raise funds. Routinely, congressional hopefuls spend more than half their time fundraising. More alarming, the pace scarcely slackens when the election is over. Freshman House members are urged to fundraise furiously as soon as they arrive. Of the top ten House fundraisers in 2007, four were wizened party leaders—and six were freshmen still finding their way to the washroom.[99]

This entire fundraising frenzy largely pays for something that is free or subsidized in nearly every other democracy. Candidates, parties, and interest groups spent $1.7 billion on TV ads for the 2006 election.[100] In 2008, the total is expected to top $5 billion. The Internet, cable TV, and other forms of "viral marketing" hardly have made a dent. Candidates still buy thirty-second ads on local television stations. Such ads are a major source of revenue for broadcasters, since candidates are a captive and often desperate market segment, willing to pay top dollar for the precious spot next to the evening news. The result is a system that too often chokes off competition and shuts ordinary voters out of the process.

And of course, money tilts policy. On deeply felt issues such as abortion or the Iraq War, campaign money would sway few. But most issues are not so morally charged. They aren't black or white; they're a shade of grey. Congress mostly considers arcane economic topics that pit industry against industry, with the public barely aware and hardly represented. On those matters, access can lead to outcomes. And politicians naturally weigh the impact of voting for or against an interest that could pour hundreds of thousands of dollars into the next election, perhaps even creating a competitive race where none exists. As Rep. Barney Frank, chair of the House Financial Services Committee, repeatedly has said, "We are the only people in the world required by law to take large amounts of money from strangers and then act as if it has no effect on our behavior."[101]

Under Texas Rep. Tom Delay, from 1995 to 2006 the House Majority Whip and then Majority Leader, the trading of cash for policy reached a level of explicit vulgarity not seen since the Gilded Age. When the GOP won the Congress in 1994, Delay summoned lobbyists to his office and showed them their names on lists deeming them "Friendly" or "Unfriendly" based on whether they gave campaign contributions only to the GOP. "If you want to play in our revolution," he told them, "you've got to play by our rules."[102] Lawmakers organized the "K Street Project," named after the Washington, D.C. street where lobbying firms often set up shop. The scheme sought to force industries to hire only Republicans for top lobbying jobs. The lobbying community became a part of the leadership machine. Key industries went from splitting their contributions to pouring twice as much money to Republicans as to Democrats. One journalist observed, "K Street used to be a barrier to sweeping change in Washington. The GOP has turned it into a weapon."[103]

At the same time, the lobbying complex itself has grown in size and impact. Lobbying is hardly new. The right to petition Congress is protected by the First Amendment. But as with so many other things, what was once a picturesque nuisance has exploded into an overwhelming phenomenon that prevents Congress from acting. The number of registered lobbyists in Washington, D.C., has *tripled* in the past decade.[104] Even more relevant, spending on lobbying has gone up by two-thirds.[105] Since 1998, nearly half of former members of Congress stayed in Washington, D.C., to become registered lobbyists.[106] Awash in money, swarmed by former colleagues making more than they do, working in a boomtown of new high-end restaurants and office buildings, lawmakers fell prey to ancient temptations. One, Rep. Duke Cunningham, offered a written list of bribes sought and what government policy could be expected. Another, William Jefferson, kept $90,000 in cash in his freezer. But the most common (and in many ways most valuable) thing that lobbyists can offer lawmakers is campaign fundraising and contributions.

Of course, we expect industries to have a loud voice in the economic policies of a capitalist democracy. But the money—the campaign giving, the lobbying, the absence of a counterbalance—can yield severe distortions. Consider the case of the pharmaceutical industry. As Congress began to mull whether it would offer a prescription drug benefit for senior citizens who receive Medicare, industry campaign contributions to congressional candidates more than doubled in four years to $30 million in 2002. Where the industry previously had spread its gifts among both parties, now it bet overwhelmingly on Republicans.[107] The complex legislation was dramatically influenced by massive lobbying, augmented by the partisan tilt of campaign funds. For example, one key provision blocked federal agencies from negotiating lower drug prices by taking advantage of its buying in bulk.[108] The overall bill appeared to lose steam in a late-night roll call on the House floor, but then House leaders held the vote open through the early morning. They threatened the political campaign of the son of one wavering lawmaker and eked out a win. Rep. Billy Tauzin of Louisiana, then the chair of the Energy and Commerce Committee, steered the pharmaceutical industry's measures through Congress. After the law was signed, Tauzin resigned his seat in Congress, and pocketed a reported $2 million per year, as the new head of the drug companies' lobbying group.[109]

In 2006, the Democrats took control of both houses of Congress. It remains to be seen whether they retain the reformist mind-set of opposition, or are more keen to reap the campaign finance rewards of incumbency.

Some signs are promising. Lawmakers began by outlawing the K Street Project, and similar schemes, in rules changes enacted on both sides of Capitol Hill that contained important legislative process improvements. In September 2007, they enacted, and the president signed into law, new rules to limit the influence of special-interest lobbyists. But core problems, such as how to address the many flaws in how electoral winners are funded and chosen, still remain to be solved.

Other signs are discouraging. Access still appears to lead to influence. In the fall of 2007, Congress began to consider a bill making clear that the Bush administration had exceeded the law in its program of warrantless domestic wiretapping. One senator, Jay Rockefeller (D-WV), earlier had handwritten a letter to Vice-President Cheney expressing concern about the legality of the program. As Congress began to craft legislation, major telephone companies worried that they would be held accountable for illegal acts that they may have committed. From 2000 until the end of 2005, Verizon and AT&T and their executives had given Rockefeller a total of $4050 in campaign contributions. In the first ten months of 2007, though, the firms' executives gave more than $42,000. After that, Rockefeller's bill quietly granted the firms immunity, noted an exposé in *Wired*.[110]

The Constitutional Con

How did we get in such a mess? Be on the lookout for men in black robes. As with any statutes or actions of the government, campaign finance laws must be constitutional, as determined by the courts. Over three decades, the U.S. Supreme Court has issued a series of decisions at odds with the best notions of the First Amendment and democracy. In few other realms has the Court so cheerily struck down laws more vitally needed and as carefully considered by the legislative branch.

From the early part of the twentieth century forward, campaign finance laws limited both spending and contributions. It seemed self-evident that the law could try to regulate the conduct of campaigns so that one side didn't drown out the other. (Those laws rarely were enforced. Still, few doubted their constitutionality.)[111] After Watergate and its revelations of campaign finance abuses, Congress passed a strong new law over President Nixon's veto. It limited candidates' spending on campaigns, capped the size of campaign contributions, and provided voluntary public financing for presidential candidates. Any law passed by

Congress must be consistent with the Constitution, and the Supreme Court issued a 762-page opinion on campaign finance, *Buckley v. Valeo.* It knocked out half the new law, left the other half hanging precariously, and set campaign practices veering off on their current course.

To the justices who ruled in *Buckley,* campaign spending and contributions are both forms of speech. Money, as the saying goes, talks. These activities are thus covered by the First Amendment and its protections of freedoms of association and expression. And any law that limits such protected speech must withstand a test of "exacting scrutiny."

According to the justices, laws can try to curb corruption and the appearance of corruption. Hence, Congress could cap the size of contributions to candidates, within reason. But government can't limit overall campaign spending just because such limits might be good for democracy, or because they would ensure one side can't drown out another, or because they are good for voters. The Court said, "the concept that government may restrict the speech of some elements of our society in order to enhance the relative voice of others is wholly foreign to the First Amendment, which was designed to secure the widest possible dissemination of information from diverse and antagonistic sources, and to assure unfettered interchange of ideas for the bringing about of political and social changes desired by the people."[112] So the Court struck down spending limits. More, since you can't corrupt yourself, the Court reasoned, Congress can't pass a law that limits what an individual can spend on his own campaign. And since the improper influence is minimal if an expenditure is not coordinated with the candidate, such independent expenditures couldn't be capped or banned, either.

The result was the system we have today: unlimited spending, with candidates forced to raise the sums in relatively small discrete amounts, and to compete in a campaign arms race, all the while worried that a bored millionaire will decide to "self-finance" and pay for his own campaign. The Supreme Court's decision was, in truth, almost perfectly at odds with the way the real world worked.

One justice, at least, was firmly rooted in that real world. Justice Byron "Whizzer" White was the only member of the Court who had ever played a substantial role in an electoral campaign (White ran John F. Kennedy's Colorado State effort in 1960). His foreboding dissent warned of the mess the Court would make by striking down spending limits. "There are many illegal ways of spending money to influence elections," he wrote. "One would be blind to history to deny that unlimited money tempts people to spend it on whatever money can buy to influence an election." He knew, too, how much time fundraising took away from the work of governing, and thus wanted to uphold spending limits. "I regret that the Court has returned them all to the treadmill."[113]

For a quarter century, the Court's lopsided constitutional doctrine guided campaign finance laws and the ways campaigns run. We remain the only Western democracy where a court's interpretation of free speech doctrine has blocked the governments from passing vital changes in campaign law. (To cite just one example, U.S. campaign spending in 2006 was fifteen times what the five major German parties spent on legislative elections the year before.)[114] But within the framework—contribution limits are permissible, spending limits are not—the Court for the most part has upheld laws designed to keep the system from spinning fully out of control.

In the most significant recent case, *McConnell v. FEC,* the Court approved the 2002 Bipartisan Campaign Reform Act (BCRA), popularly known after its team of Senate sponsors, Republican John McCain and Democrat Russell Feingold.[115] The Court gave a green light to the bill's two key provisions. The first banned "soft money" donations to parties. Soft money, the term for unlimited and often undisclosed contributions to parties from otherwise illegal sources such as corporate and union treasuries, or in huge amounts from individuals, threatened to overwhelm the entire system. It had been illegal for candidates to receive contributions directly from corporations since 1907.[116] Politicians had discovered over time that while they couldn't raise large sums for themselves, they could steer unlimited funds to their own political parties, which in turn could buy TV ads and otherwise run what any layperson would think was a campaign for a candidate. By 2000, such unlimited corporate contributions to parties dwarfed the total amounts given to presidential candidates themselves. It was, to paraphrase crafty Lyndon Johnson, "more loophole than law." The 2002 change plugged the loophole and restored some semblance of limits. Candidates were prohibited from steering tens of millions of dollars in otherwise illegal gifts to the Republican or Democratic Party. The system was hardly purified, but the worst abuses were cut off. The Court agreed that this was an acceptable way to stop the circumvention of campaign finance laws.

At first, the Court also upheld the new law's other key plank. Over the years, economic interest groups, especially corporations, found that they could spend unlimited sums on "issue ads." These ads usually were aimed squarely at a candidate for office; they were often harsh and even vituperative; they aired up to the moment the polls opened; and they could be paid for in unlimited amounts by corporations who would be barred from making campaign contributions or even directly spending the money on campaign ads. So long as the ads did not specifically say "vote for" or "vote against" a candidate, the law treated them the same as a lone citizen standing on a street corner handing out flyers on global warming.

In fact, as a Brennan Center study showed, these were phony issue ads, the vast majority of them actually directed at campaigns. Nonparty groups aired at least $98 million of sham issue ads in 2000, most in the weeks just before the election.[117] Three quarters of issue ads were negative, while candidate ads were overwhelmingly positive in tone—plainly, candidates are happier playing "good cop" so their image isn't sullied by wielding the billy club. In a typical example, a group called Voters for Campaign Truth ran "issue" ads in South Carolina during the 2000 GOP primary demanding, "John McCain, stop this bigoted attack on the Christian voters of South Carolina and America."[118]

The McCain–Feingold law said that if an ad was broadcast in a candidate's district within sixty days before an election or thirty days before a primary contest, and mentioned (usually lancing) the candidate, it is electioneering, not an issue ad. That meant that the ads couldn't be funded directly out of corporate or labor union treasuries, and that the public had to be told who paid for them. The Court upheld that provision in *McConnell,* too. It left open the possibility for groups to challenge the law as it was applied, rather than just asking whether it's constitutional on its face, much like an author leaving a dangling plot line ready for the sequel.

Ominously, the *McConnell* ruling was 5–4.[119] Within three years, two young new conservative justices had joined the Court: John Roberts and Samuel Alito. Now 5–4 had become 4–5.

In June 2007, the Court ruled on the matter of "sham issue ads" again.[120] A group of anti-abortion activists, Wisconsin Right to Life, tried to run ads attacking Sen. Russell Feingold's position on judicial nominations during his reelection campaign. The ads were run while the Senate was in recess and could not vote on judicial nominees, but they were not run once Senator Feingold won reelection and the filibuster again became an issue. From the bench, Justice Stephen Breyer told the lawyer for the anti-abortion group, "If we agree with you in this case, goodbye McCain–Feingold."[121] The case technically only applied to this set of facts. But the Court in effect ruled that corporations and unions were exempt from the "electioneering" provisions of the law, unless the ads were "the functional equivalent of express advocacy."[122] This is little more comprehensible to constitutional lawyers than to anyone else. Though the justices ruled only on this particular case, in fact, the implications loom larger.

In practical terms, thanks to the Court's ruling, we will likely see tens of millions of dollars of sham issue ads paid for by corporations and unions once again clogging the airwaves in the weeks before Election Day. The 2008 election will likely be a clamorous swamp of special-interest money.

Professor Rick Hasen of Loyola Law School, a leading election law expert, wrote of the recent sham ad case, "The pendulum has swung sharply away from Supreme Court deference to campaign finance regulation toward perhaps the greatest period of deregulation" since well before Watergate.[123] Vermont passed a far-reaching campaign financing law that put in place public financing for campaigns for governor. At the same time, Vermont imposed a mandatory campaign spending limit, arguing that the Court in *Buckley* didn't foresee the explosive arms race of fundraising—which has had an inevitably corrupting impact, as candidates vie for funds from people seeking to influence legislation. That argument is profoundly correct, and in fact the Justice Department prepared to take that position during the Clinton administration. But the Court shrugged off the spending limits proposal.[124] Stripped to its core, the justices in effect ruled, *Can't you read? We said no spending limits.* That was no surprise. But the Vermont law did something else, too: it limited individual contributions to a candidate (ranging from $200 to $400) through a primary and general election. These would appear to be the kind of corruption-fighting caps that the Court repeatedly has upheld. In fact, in the previous three decades the Court never once had struck down a contribution limit.[125] There's a first time for everything. In 2006 Vermont's limit on contributions was deemed to be simply too low, and the state hadn't shown any "special justification" why it needed these low limits. Several justices wanted to strike down any limits at all. After all, they reasoned, why can a state decide that $1000 is the maximum, but not $500 or $100?

The Rise of Small-donor Democracy

There is one bright sign: the sudden rise of small contributions from individuals, millions of Americans who never before gave to a political candidate or party, who now find it easy to do so through the tap of a keypad.

This new phenomenon was a hoped-for consequence of McCain–Feingold, which ended the soft money system. In the 1990s, the parties had grown dependent upon these ever-larger contributions. The Republican Party also built a massive list of individual, largely conservative donors, but the Democrats let their individual donor base atrophy. When McCain–Feingold cut off the soft money raised by parties, the Democrats and Republicans had no choice but to turn to individuals. From about 2003 on, individual giving surged. In 2000 the Democrats had raised $275 million in "hard" money from individual donors; by 2004, they had raised $679 million.[126] The GOP, in turn, that year raised $782 million from individuals.

This detonation of small-donor democracy was amplified enormously by the Internet. In years past, it was especially expensive to raise funds from numerous donors through fundraising cocktail parties or direct mail. Appeals to wealthy individuals for large gifts steered to political parties were more cost effective. Now, suddenly, it cost even less to raise millions from tens of thousands of donors. Economists talk about "friction-free capitalism" that cuts out transaction costs; this was friction-free politics.

The first hint came in 2000, when Sen. John McCain won a surprise victory in the New Hampshire Republican primary. Within two days, he raised nearly $1 million online, and had raised $5 million by the time he suspended his campaign a month later. Four years after, Howard Dean's presidential campaign raised over $20 million from online donors.[127] Less publicized, but even more lucrative, John Kerry's campaign raised over $82 million.[128] The 2008 presidential candidates tapped an even deeper pool of donors. In the first six months of 2007, Barack Obama raised $58 million from 258,000 donors, $17.2 million of it culled online.[129] Of Obama's 100,000 Internet donors during that time, nine out of ten gave less than $100. In January 2008, he raised $28 million online. In one quarter, Hillary Clinton raised $4 million in individual contributions less than $200 each.[130] Republican Ron Paul raised $4.07 million in one day online.[131] It was a revolution in political fundraising.[132]

Small donors can be best swayed by a sharper ideological appeal, and one could imagine this trend driving the parties to their extremes. Even if true, that is far better than a political fundraising system rooted in cash-for-policy extracted from a few big economic interests. Already, presidential campaigns are recalibrating their fundraising strategy to boost their take from mass solicitation, as are congressional campaign committees. Individual candidates (who have a harder time building lists) may soon follow suit. And this Internet fundraising culture may in turn be the root of reform that could make a big difference.

Groundhog Day for Reform

Reform has proven so elusive for so long that it is easy to give up hope; it can feel like the Bill Murray movie *Groundhog Day*. Put another way, you can't lose money over time betting against campaign finance reform. The politics of change can be excruciatingly hard. Lawmakers think not as Democrats or as Republicans, but as incumbents.

The most recent serious chance for basic reform came in 1993. Ross Perot had run for president and pounded on the need to curb lobbyists and special-interest influence, and he won one out of every five votes. On Election Night, before thirty thousand people in Little Rock, President Elect Clinton declared that he heard the message from the electorate, and that he would fight for reform. A few days later, he announced that campaign finance reform would be one of his four top priorities. At the dining room table in the governor's mansion, as movers scurried about packing for the move to Washington, he dictated a passage for his Inaugural Address, aimed at the fellow dignitaries on the platform. "I say to all of us here, let us resolve to reform our politics, so that power and privilege no longer shout down the voice of the people."

It was a deceptively serene tableau when Clinton and Vice-President Gore met privately with the Democratic leaders for their first meeting in office, around the grand table in the Cabinet Room. The topic was campaign reform. Clinton urged change, as did Gore. Senate Democrats forcefully agreed. Then Speaker of the House Tom Foley spoke in the coded language of power. What he *said* was encouraging. The Democrats in the House are for reform, he said. They would get it done. Then he added offhandedly that "it will be hard for Rosty [tax writing committee chairman Dan Rostenkowski] to whip the guys on this and the tax bill at the same time, but he'll do it." What he *meant* was: *If you dare to push this on us, rookie, we will mess with your tax bill, your top priority, so badly you won't know what hit you.* It was like a scene from a gangster movie. The new president slumped slightly in his seat.

Later that year, the House and Senate did pass companion bills that limited spending, instituted partial public financing, and banned the unlimited "soft money" contributions that had flooded the presidential campaign. It was a strong plan. Then neither chamber appointed members of the conference committee that could write a final compromise plan. For a full year, nothing happened. Reformers stymied the measure, in part, because they insisted on minutely calibrated limits on gifts from political action committees and complex rules governing fundraising by so-called "bundlers" who gathered checks from individuals. Meanwhile, lawmakers were happy to do nothing. The House Democrats' top political strategist privately insisted flatly, "If we pass reform, we will lose the House." As the election approached, lawmakers realized with a start that voters were furious, and they scrambled to bring the bill to a final vote. By then, the Republicans mounted a filibuster. But they were busy shooting a corpse. Campaign finance reform was already dead.[133]

How to avoid similar mistakes? The next wave of reform will stop focusing just on capping spending and gifts. It will center not exclusively on such ceilings but on building a floor: a strong platform so candidates can make their case, and voters will have a real choice, based on the merits of the argument and not just on the ability to raise enough money to be heard.

Many reformers have begun to look honestly at the successes and failures of their movement. Too often, campaign finance reform has been presented as a hygienic response to politics: "Clean up Congress." Get rid of "dirty money." Campaign reform must recognize that the problem with politics is not that it costs a lot of money—in fact, we may want *more* money in politics, if it kindles citizen engagement. The problem is not the volume of funds, but that the way the money is raised—both who gives, and how the money chase leads inevitably to corruption. Today's system freezes out ordinary citizens—one more barrier to broad democratic participation. We'll never purge money out of politics. But we can empower millions of citizens to have the loudest voice in the system. Let's see how to do this.

FAIR ELECTIONS THROUGH FULL PUBLIC FUNDING

The most sweeping change that could be made in our elections is to enact public financing of elections. Simply, candidates who gather a threshold of support—such as in small contributions—would receive a public grant to pay for their campaigns in exchange for limiting their spending. They would not have to spend endless months fundraising or kowtowing to donors for large contributions. This change would not add new fundraising rules, or try to limit the spending of wealthy individuals. What it would do is give candidates the chance to run, if they want, accountable to the broad population of voters rather than the narrow band of donors.

Public funding responds most directly to so many of the problems bedeviling politics today. It would free candidates, including incumbents, to focus on policy and on retail politics, rather than on endless rounds of fundraising. It would literally add weeks of substantive work time to the calendars of elected officials, who now schedule their floor votes and hearings so as not to preempt needed time for contacting donors.

It would put ordinary citizens far more directly at the center of politics, as well. Money may speak, but only relatively few citizens have the wherewithal to be heard. In the

2004 elections, less than 0.6 percent of voting-age Americans gave a candidate more than $200, the threshold for public disclosure of donors.[134]

At the same time, public funding is good for electoral competition. Incumbents, not challengers, today have easy access to legislatively interested money. Foes charge that public funding helps incumbents and the wealthy (whose spending is not limited). If it really benefited incumbents and the wealthy, wouldn't it have become law long ago? After all, we had a working system of public funding in place for presidential elections from 1976 until about 2000. When the system was in place, challengers beat incumbent presidents in three out of seven contests. Few congressional districts boast that much competition. (By contrast, in the rest of the twentieth century, incumbent presidents lost only twice.)[135] Make no mistake, when the TV lights are off, lawmakers scoff at the idea that reform helps incumbents. During haggling over a proposed public funding bill, the House Democrats' top negotiator blurted out, "You don't get it! We're not *about* helping challengers!"

This approach also sidesteps many constitutional issues that have tripped up campaign giving and spending limits. Any spending limits are voluntary. In *Buckley v. Valeo,* the Court said the presidential funding system "is a congressional effort, not to abridge, restrict, or censor speech, but rather to use public money to facilitate and enlarge public discussion and participation in the electoral process, goals vital to a self-governing people."

Public financing is an old idea whose time has come. Theodore Roosevelt first urged it in 1907. "The need for collecting large campaign funds would vanish if Congress provided an appropriation for the proper and legitimate expenses of each of the great national parties," he said in a Message to Congress.[136] After the Watergate scandal, public funding was instituted for presidential races from 1976 forward. When the Republicans or Democrats had chosen their nominee at their convention, from that point on the candidate could not accept private funds, and would receive a grant from taxpayers. The system worked for several decades. Eventually, though, the amount of money available for candidates proved too small given the huge sums that could be raised by candidates who did not participate. In part, the grant was set too low. As law professor Samuel Isaccharoff has pointed out, it was pegged at roughly two-thirds of the amount spent by the 1972 presidential bid of George McGovern, who lost in a historic landslide; in other words, it was two-thirds of the *least successful* presidential campaign in modern history.[137] At the same time, over the years the number of citizens agreeing on their tax returns to check off three dollars for public funding is steadily drop-ping. Few voters understand that their taxes do not go up when they check the box; more, they don't really know what the checkoff funds are used for. A candidate who limited her spending could get swamped by a nonparticipating candi-date's ads during the weeks between the two party's conven-tions. By 2004, neither John Kerry nor George Bush took public funding for the primaries. In 2008, among major-party candidates, only John Edwards opted to seek matching funds. He didn't receive kudos when he did.

Congressional attempts to pass public funding foundered on the sense that the public, far from clamoring for it, would punish politicians who voted yes. Opponents successfully filibustered public funding in 1993 and 1994. Talk show hosts easily derided the plan as "welfare for politicians." To pass the urgent emergency measures to clamp down on soft money, the controversial taxpayer subsidies were jettisoned. The McCain–Feingold law included no public monies.

But while the presidential system crumbled, without fanfare, states around the country began to build their own public funding systems. They found a way to construct the measures that were modern, modest in cost, and that garnered broad public support.

- In conservative Arizona, races for governor and state legislature now are publicly financed. Six of eight statewide winning candidates participated in the system. Governor Janet Napolitano was among them. "I got to spend time with voters as opposed to dialing for dollars, or trying to sell tickets to $250-a-plate fundraisers," the Democrat later enthused. "This was much better." A Republican state senator recalled, "Under the old system I'd be in my office dialing for dollars. I'd spend most of the campaign raising money. Under Clean Elections [the name of the Arizona system], I got my qualifying contributions, and I did it not by hanging out at the country club or sitting on the telephone dialing the wealthy. I went to union halls, to the A.M.E. Church in downtown Phoenix, where a Republican had not been seen in 20 years; I went to places all over Arizona. Under the old system, three zip codes accounted for 90 percent of the campaign contributions. Under clean elections, [the people who gave small qualifying gifts] were spread across the state. There was an energization of the electorate. People felt their vote mattered."[138]

- Maine voters passed their version of Clean Elections by referendum in 1996 for governor, state senator, and state representative.[139] By a decade later, eight of ten candidates participated, limiting their spending and accepting public funds.[140] Deborah Simpson was a single mother juggling a job waiting tables and college. Using the public funding system, she was elected to the legislature.

- In Connecticut, the governor left office in an unusual way: within months, he went to prison. His successor, Republican Jodi Rell, worked with the Democratic legislature to pass the first full public funding system covering the legislature passed by lawmakers themselves, rather than imposed on them by voters.

Now, for the first time in nearly two decades, members of Congress are gearing up once again to press for public financing. Senators Richard Durbin, Democrat of Illinois, and Arlen Specter, Republican of Pennsylvania, have proposed a voluntary plan for Senate elections. What they call their Fair Elections Now Act would mark a remarkable shift in American politics. Here's how it would work. Candidates would have to amass contributions from small donors, limited to $100 a person and as low as $5. If they amassed several thousand of these gifts, then they qualify for public funding, enough to run their campaign up to a spending limit. No more fundraising, no spending of personal fortunes, period. Candidates who participate would be eligible for "Fair Fight Funds" if they face a free-spending opponent or massive independent expenditures by outside groups. This would match the spending of foes, dollar for dollar, enough to double the participating candidate's spending. Among other things, this will make it more likely that candidates will opt in to participating in the voluntary system. The Durbin–Specter bill would pay for this mostly by assessing fees on the very broadcasters who get paid such a large share of campaign costs. Overall, the program would cost about $1.75 billion per two-year election cycle.

The greatest appeal of Fair Elections is its simplicity and the way it eliminates the constant search for funds. Once qualifying contributions are collected, candidates do not have to raise another dime. They can carry their message to voters, without dunning them for donations.

This approach bears a substantive and political risk, though. The public may have internalized the notion that contributing to a candidate is an exuberant example of free expression, not just nascent corruption. Is there any way to improve the proposed public financing system to create incentives for more participation, more organizing, and greater involvement of ordinary citizens? There is one possibility, and it's in the Big Apple.

IF YOU CAN MAKE IT THERE...

It's hard to shock a New Yorker, of course. But in 1986, Gotham was mesmerized by a scandal designed for tabloid headlines. The Queens borough president was found in his car, bleeding, claiming he had been kidnapped and attacked. It soon became clear he had slit his wrists. A scandal spilled out, involving kickbacks, graft, campaign corruption, and the city's Parking Violations Bureau. Weeks later, he killed himself with a kitchen knife.[141] Soon many of the city's top Democratic politicians were headed to jail. Mayor Ed Koch, not corrupt himself but embarrassed by entanglement with crooked party leaders, pressed for a reform that would save his reputation and the city's image. New York created a municipal public financing system.

New York's scheme does not pretend to end all private fundraising. Rather, it hugely boosts the impact of small individual giving. Small contributions of $250 or less are matched by taxpayer funds—four dollars for every dollar given. So a subway conductor's contribution of $50 would become $250. A $250 gift becomes $1250. In the future, small contributions will receive a six-to-one match. Candidates who participate must limit their spending and must appear in debates. New York also imposes term limits on all officeholders.

All these laws have led to an eruption of political competition. Candidates organize their campaigns through dozens of house parties, small fundraisers in people's homes that are accessible and affordable for the vast majority of the city's residents. It has enabled a crop of diverse and talented officials to run, most of whom would never have sought elective office otherwise.

Eric Gioia was a twenty-seven-year-old lawyer when he first ran for the New York City Council. He grew up above his family's florist shop in Queens, worked as a janitor to pay his way through law school, and while he had worked in the White House for President Clinton, he had no base in local politics and no money to speak of. Gioia took full advantage of the matching fund system and won a City Council seat in a hotly contested election. "When I ran, no part of the Democratic Party establishment supported me. To run in Queens without that support was virtually impossible. The things that made it possible were the campaign finance system, especially the four to one match, and the Internet," he recalls. "I ran a campaign where I was going stoop to stoop and living room to living room—and those twenty buck contributions really add up." Gioia represents the most ethnically diverse district in New York, and still uses the Internet to invite people to fundraisers with no specific cover charge. "It's a combination of a fundraiser and a MeetUp," he says. "I have found that grassroots fundraising becomes grassroots organizing becomes a political coalition and then a governing coalition." Now Gioia is using the same techniques to run for citywide office.[142]

We can imagine a proposal for presidential or congressional reform that would be, simply, four-to-one-matching funds plus a voluntary spending limit. For high-profile races where donors give through the Internet, such a system would be a booster rocket for participation and impact. It would create powerful incentives to campaigns to churn more support from more people. At the very least, it could change the Fair Elections proposal by letting candidates continue to raise very small contributions, even after receiving the big public grant, and even having those contributions be matched.

IF ALL ELSE FAILS, CHANGE THE CONSTITUTION

Neither public funding system can stop millionaires or the stray billionaire from buying office. When Michael Bloomberg ran for mayor of New York, he didn't participate in the matching fund system, to put it mildly. Bloomberg spent a total of $99 per vote to win the New York mayoralty in 2001; by contrast, that same year Ken Livingstone spent 80 cents per vote to become mayor of London. All told, Bloomberg spent $158 million to get and keep his job.[143]

The Supreme Court has made plain that it is unlikely to allow spending limits. Arguments can be made, even under the pretzel logic of *Buckley v. Valeo*—most strongly, that the money chase forces politicians to crave cash, all of which is an incentive for corruption. Powerful arguments: but if the Court disagrees, irrelevant.

Should the Supreme Court in coming cases lurch away from allowing campaign finance regulation altogether, then a crisis will have been reached and states should consider a constitutional amendment. Such an ammendment could make clear that nothing in the Constitution should prevent Congress from passing a law limiting spending by a campaign, including campaigns funded by the candidate themselves. Such a proposal got forty Senate votes in 2001. Senators Charles Schumer (D-NY) and Arlen Specter (R-PA) introduced an amendment in 2007.[144] Among other things, constitutional spending limits would take away the risk of a free-spending wealthy foe, one of the main reasons incumbent politicians fear public funding. On the other hand, some argue that we will only enact public funding (which many politicians dread) if it is part of a package with voluntary spending limits (which they crave). Perhaps, but over thirty years after *Buckley,* such an inducement has hardly been an overwhelming gravitational force for reform.

Again, such a constitutional change may be needed if the Court goes even further to undermine needed reform. But equally bold change is possible, now, under *current* constitutional doctrine. Public funding could pass immediately. Lawmakers ought not use the prospect of a constitutional amendment, far harder to enact, as an excuse to avoid immediate and positive change.

5

GERRYMANDERING

What It Is, and Why It Matters More Than You Think

Gerrymandering is a funny word with a serious impact. In his *Political Dictionary,* William Safire defines it succinctly as the "drawing of political lines by the party in power so as to perpetuate its power."[145] Flagrant gerrymandering is today's unspoken political reality. The United States is unique in regularly redrawing electoral district lines—and in having those legislative lines drawn by the legislators themselves.

Today, few congressional districts are competitive. The 2002 election, concluded three leading law professors who studied the issue, was the least competitive in American history.[146] A true electoral tide may still swamp incumbents, but it would have to be at *S.S. Poseidon* strength. For example, in 2006 the Democrats would likely have won a dozen more seats had district lines been drawn differently. Routinely, voters don't choose lawmakers—lawmakers choose voters.

To be sure, gerrymandering is as old as the republic. In the very first Congress, none other than Patrick Henry tried to draw electoral lines to keep James Madison from being elected.[147] The word "gerrymander" comes from a congressional district approved by Massachusetts governor Elbridge Gerry in 1812, which resembled a salamander. (Famous painter Gilbert Stuart drew the cartoon map.)[148] In the early 1980s, legendary California Democratic congressman Phil Burton held court at Frank Fat's Chinese restaurant in Sacramento, negotiating and redrawing the Golden State's district lines. Democrats gained five seats. Burton wryly called the electoral map his "contribution to modern art."[149]

THE GERRY-MANDER.

But after the 1990 and especially after the 2000 census, the exceptional gerrymander became the norm. As Juliet Elipren points out in *Fight Club Politics,* when Phil Burton drew his creative maps, he assessed what kind of voters lived in various neighborhoods by the crude measure of what cars residents drove. (Volvos, wealthy Democrats. Buicks, middle-class Republicans. Chevys, middle-class Democrats.)[150] Now, with powerful new districting software based on census data, it has become far easier to draw lines to favor one party or another, or to favor incumbents of both flavors.

In 2002, eighty-one congressional incumbents faced no major-party opponent.[151] In 2004, when the incumbent president narrowly beat his challenger, all but ten House victors won easily, the vast majority of them in landslides.[152] Because most districts now are truly one-party fiefdoms, the real battles often rage in primaries, which pull lawmakers to the ideological fringe—and, in any event, give hundreds of members of Congress the serenity of knowing that their views or votes will never get them punished electorally. In some states, parties have linked arms to protect incumbents. In California in 2002, after the U.S. Census, not a single incumbent Member of Congress lost. Law professor Samuel Issacharoff calls this a "political cartel."

Parties grow increasingly brazen as they grapple for advantage. In Georgia, serpentine lines and multimember districts meant that even though the Republicans won 55 percent of the vote for state senators, they won only 45 percent of the seats. In 2002, when Georgia voters rejected a Democratic incumbent senator and governor, Democrats actually gained two U.S. House seats. Republicans had Georgia on their minds when they in turn, gerrymandered Pennsylvania. "Pennsylvania will make Georgia look like a picnic," the head of the House Republican campaign committee vowed.[153] Meanwhile, Michigan lost a single House seat in the 2000 election, but Republican state legislators managed to draw lines that crammed six Democratic incumbent congressmen into three districts.[154] In Florida, one congressional district is 90 miles long and no more than 3 miles wide. "It consists of every beach house lining Route A1A along Florida's Gold Coast from West Palm Beach to Miami Beach," reports the *Economist* magazine. "You could say about this district ... that you could kill most of the constituents by driving down the road with the car doors open."[155]

Borders of propriety, always faint, have been erased. The most notorious example came in Texas. Two years after the 2000 U.S. Census, Republicans gained control of both legislative chambers. The appropriate step would have been to wait for the next census to redraw the lines. Rep. Tom Delay—then at peak power as House Majority Leader—had other ideas. In the summer of 2003, a special session of the legislature was called to push through mid-decade redistricting. Delay flew back from Washington several times to oversee the effort. He also raised millions of dollars in corporate funds for a political committee to back the redistricting plan.[156]

Democrats realized they lacked the votes to block the change outright. They bolted. Dozens of state legislators fled to Oklahoma and New Mexico, all in an effort to deny a quorum (enough lawmakers present to have a binding vote). The federal Department of Homeland Security was enlisted to join the search for "the Killer Ds." Eventually, enough of them trickled back to Austin to allow the plan to pass. The state's congressional delegation flipped from being 17–15 Democratic to 18–16 Republican.[157]

As a matter of impressively raw politics, the drive was plainly effective. It was also illegal. In 2005, Delay and three of his top aides were indicted for their efforts. The indictments charged that the men improperly funneled millions of dollars from corporations to candidates in the redistricting push. Delay eventually resigned from Congress and awaits trial. In the meantime, the GOP electoral gains remained in the law.

The Courts Step In, and Out

Many had hoped the courts would step in to help right this situation. Since the early 1960s, the Supreme Court has wrestled with how to give voters a true voice. In *Baker v. Carr* and *Reynolds v. Sims,* the Court waded into the "political thicket" and ruled that each legislative district must have essentially the same number of people as other districts. That would equalize the voice of voters. (Hence, "one person, one vote.") Yet the justices furrowed their brows repeatedly over the years, puzzling over exactly what role they should and should not take in crafting such districts.

The Texas case seemed the best opportunity for clarity, precisely because it concerned such naked opportunism: a mid-decade redistricting, conducted for purely partisan reasons, explicitly to use the process to boost one party over another. If this didn't violate the Constitution's equal protection clause, it was hard to see what would. In 2006, in *LULAC v. Perry,* the Court simply washed its hands of the challenge.[158] It struck down one district because it violated the Voting Rights Act, but found no constitutional problem with one party pushing through a new overall redistricting plan in the middle of the decade solely to squeeze in a few more seats. In theory, there's no reason redistricting couldn't happen every time the major parties swap control. Candidates will routinely choose voters, rather than the other way around. Now it's up to the political process to fix itself.

Hasta la Vista, Baby

In fact, gerrymandering reform has become a hot topic in several states. Most measures would remove the job of setting lines from legislatures, and give the job to a nonpartisan commission. That's how it is done in Iowa. There, a panel of nonpartisan experts produces up to three maps for the legislature to vote up or down. Iowa has only five members of Congress, but even in 2002, the state had three competitive races.[159] In Arizona, hundreds of thousands of citizens signed a petition for "Fair Districts, Fair Elections" to take the power away from legislators alone. Now, state lawmakers will pick a panel from a group of independent citizens who volunteer.

In 2005, Governor Arnold Schwarzenegger sought a ballot initiative to create a redistricting commission for California. Retired judges would have filled the panel. His rationale: the existing map was drawn to benefit incumbents of both parties, but a fairer map would likely have hurt Democrats. In Ohio, meanwhile, the Republicans who controlled the governorship and both houses of the legislature were consumed by scandals. Reformers forced a measure onto the ballot, which would create a similar redistricting panel for Ohio. A fairer map there would likely have hurt Republicans. Editorial boards roared support in both states. But on Election Day, reformers got a sour surprise. The redistricting reform measure lost in Ohio by 70–30 percent, and in California the "Governator" couldn't lift the measure; it won only 40 percent of the vote. Why did voters reject reform? Strikingly, in each state, foes painted the measure as a partisan grab (for a different party in each state). Less obviously, public opinion polls showed that voters also distrusted a supposedly elitist process. In California, for example, the overwhelming number of elderly retired judges are, not surprisingly, white men.

ONE NATION, ONE STANDARD

Partisans, even when feeling twinges of guilt, thus are stuck in a classic "prisoner's dilemma," the name given to the choice faced by a suspect who isn't sure whether to squeal, and needs to know if his coconspirator has already done so. *I'll reform if you do. And you go first.* If voters in individual states rightly sense that piecemeal reform is unfair, the ultimate answer is to set national standards.

Congress could pass a law requiring states to use redistricting commissions. One of the proposed measures was introduced in 2007 by Reps. Zach Wamp, a Republican, and John Tanner, a Democrat. It requires every state to create a redistricting commission, or to have lines drawn by a federal court. It also bans mid-decade redistricting. It seems evident that a national government in the twenty-first century should have one common standard for how legislative lines are drawn.

But the *how* of redistricting is only one question. *What* is the goal of improving the way lines are drawn? Yes, we want competition, but does that mean that every race in every district must be a cliffhanger? How can we protect minority voting rights beyond the minimal protections now afforded by the Voting Rights Act? How important is it that districts are small—does it matter if everyone in a town votes for the same member of Congress? These questions lack obvious answers. And without national standards, even fifty state commissions could create a lopsided patchwork. Still, we can say forcefully that we want more competition, and that it should be possible to do this without wiping out civil rights gains that have helped ensure minority representation in Congress.

We can't let reform languish while Congress dithers. The 2010 U.S. Census looms, followed no doubt by another orgy of self-dealing. What to do? Here the nation's governors could step in, using their collective bully pulpits to catalyze change. One could imagine the National Governors Association creating a panel to conduct deep research and set out standards for redistricting. The nation's governors could jointly pledge to veto any line-drawing plans that don't follow those standards. One could imagine the Democratic governors of New York and Ohio and the Republican governors of California and Texas could link arms. This advisory panel could propose consensus, broad principles to guide the line-drawing. That could be a benchmark against which we measure state efforts. Key state governors could play a critical role.

Perhaps voters sense that reforms may need a few more minutes in the policy oven. But time is not our friend. Key tests will come after the next census, when a new crop of governors must work with legislators to craft new lines. Perhaps a national effort makes sense, so both parties jump into the unknown together. In any case, clear standards are needed, and voters must hold politicians to account. Voters must have a true choice.

Gerrymandering stands with campaign finance and vote suppression as one of the great obstacles to true democracy. Now the Supreme Court has abdicated its vital role. It's up to citizens and elected officials to fix the system, or be resigned to a system that is fixed.

6

FLUNK THE
ELECTORAL COLLEGE

Ensuring That Every Vote Actually Counts

It was the end of the long, sweltering summer at the Constitutional Convention in Philadelphia. Delegates were anxious to finish, but a big question remained: How would the new office of president be filled? One delegate wanted Congress to choose. Another wanted popular election. *That* idea was overwhelmingly voted down. It would be "unnatural," warned one foe. Southern states had extra representation in Congress because slaves were counted in the population under the grand compromise that allowed the Constitution to move forward; a popular vote would wipe out that advantage, since slaves don't vote.

The delegates referred the mess to the Committee on Details, which wrote a draft of the Constitution with the Electoral College as a rather convoluted solution. The states would each choose electors, with one electoral vote per senator and House member. That way small states, especially slave states, would have extra clout. If no one got an electoral vote majority, the House of Representatives would decide. Anyway, everyone knew George Washington would be the first president. With a shrug, the Founding Fathers moved on to other matters.[160]

The Electoral College is the exploding cigar of American politics. Four times, the candidate who won fewer votes nonetheless has become president. (Political scientists, with rare concision, call this the "wrong winner" problem.[161]) In 1824, Andrew Jackson won the most total votes, but not enough states to win the Electoral College. The House of Representatives picked John Quincy Adams instead, after a bitterly alleged "corrupt bargain" with another candidate. Then, in 1876, Democrat Samuel J. Tilden won more votes than Republican Rutherford B. Hayes, but not an Electoral College majority. The deadlocked election went to Congress. The deal: Republicans got the White House, but Democrats got federal troops pulled out of the South, ending Reconstruction and ushering in ninety years of repression against the former slaves and their descendants. In 1888, Benjamin Harrison lost the popular vote but won the Electoral College.

And in 2000, Al Gore got half a million votes more than George W. Bush, a wider popular vote margin than Kennedy had to best Nixon—but with Florida, Bush won the Electoral College by 271–266.

The Florida recount transfixed the nation. The surreal election night, with the TV networks calling first Gore and then Bush the winner. The snarled recounts, with local officials squinting at "hanging chads." The "Brooks Brothers riot" of GOP congressional staffers that shut down the counting in

Miami. Finally, the abrupt and unsigned Supreme Court intervention that stopped the counting and gave Bush the final win.

Without the melodrama, what would have shocked was simply the fact that the new president had in fact come in second in the popular vote. Indeed, just before the election, the Republicans had prepared talking points urging their adherents to say the election was illegitimate if *Gore* had prevailed without winning the most popular votes.[162]

Near misses are even more common. In 2004, Bush won the national popular vote, but a switch of 60,000 in Ohio would have elected John Kerry. In 1976, the election would have been thrown into the House of Representatives with the shift of a few thousand votes in Delaware and Ohio. Any race could turn on such flukes. And when the House chooses, each state gets one vote, giving empty Idaho the same say as crowded California. Massive pressure would push lawmakers to back the candidate of their party, not the voters. The resulting political fracas would dwarf anything seen in a century.

All that is true in a year when the system *doesn't* work—when the runner-up gets the gold medal. But the truth is, the Electoral College warps competition and subverts political equality even when it *does* work.

Because most states are reliably "red" or "blue," candidates focus nearly *all* their efforts on a few "swing" states. As a result, many voters never see a campaign ad, receive more than a perfunctory candidate visit, or experience the mass mobilization and get-out-the-vote fervor of a real campaign.

As late as 1976, forty states were tightly contested, including all the big ones. More recently, though, only about seventeen states were in play by November. As *Business Week* notes, "The corn farmer living in Iowa (one of the Sweet Seventeen) is coveted by both parties and showered with goodies such as ethanol subsidies. But just next door, the wheat grower in Republican South Dakota is insignificant to Presidential candidates. Ditto the hog farmer in Nebraska, the potato grower in Idaho, and the rancher in Oklahoma."[163]

Here is a remarkable map based on a study by the organization FairVote, chaired by former Republican presidential candidate John Anderson. In the map on the left, the "hands" represent visits by the major-party presidential and vice-presidential candidates in the final five weeks before the 2004 election. In the map on the right, dollar signs represent advertising spending by the campaigns during that time.

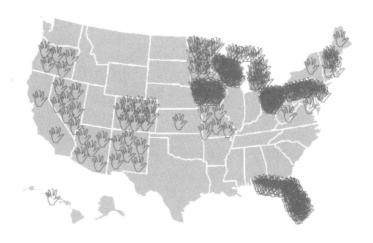

According to the group, "more money was spent on television advertising in Florida ... than in 45 states and the District of Columbia combined. More than half of all campaign resources were dedicated to just three states—Florida, Ohio and Pennsylvania." Voters in eighteen states, meanwhile, didn't get a candidate visit or a cent of spending on TV advertisements.[164]

In New York in 2004, ardent campaign boosters never dreamed of going door to door in their own neighborhoods. Instead, they packed buses and went to Pennsylvania or even, for the truly adventurous, Ohio—where they canvassed neighborhoods exactly like their own. Imagine, by contrast, a system in which every vote counted equally. Candidates would be forced to appeal to the broadest groups of voters, forced to campaign where people actually live, forced to focus on turnout.

The Electoral College is such an obvious affront to basic democracy that its backers have a hard time finding arguments to defend it. Political scientist Norman Ornstein argues, "Three (or four) crises out of more than 50 presidential elections is remarkably small."[165] Few of the assertions, even if true, are strong enough to overcome the fact that the winning candidate can lose. For example, defenders insist the system protects the power of states with less population. In a technical sense, this may be true. More accurately, though, the system protects swing states, not small states. Candidates do little campaigning in reliably Republican Idaho or Democratic Rhode Island. More, the focus on small versus large states risks confusing legal jurisdictions with actual people. States aren't living beings; people are. (As one website drolly puts it, "Dirt Don't Vote.") It is far more important that citizens have their voices heard than that states do. Gun owners or women or students or Evangelical Christians live all over the country—but only the ones in Ohio or Florida get wooed and get organized. Supporters also note that the Electoral College helps create consensus and confer legitimacy by making narrow victories seem wider than they are. True, except for when the system demolishes legitimacy by picking the wrong candidate.

For a long time, the Electoral College seemed like a quaint anachronism with little real impact, little more than a question on the citizenship test and a subject for political thriller novels. Then, of course, came the 2000 election. Now the aftermath of that contest has forced campaigns and ordinary voters to focus more on the system. Rather than taking it as a distorting given, though, we can do something about it.

CHANGE THE CONSTITUTION

Why not change the Constitution? That solution is obvious, elegant, and very hard. The greatest strides toward democracy often have come through amendments. In fact, five of the Constitutional amendments have changed who can vote and how. (Most recently, the voting age was lowered to eighteen.) But to change the charter, first the House and Senate must both pass the amendment by two-thirds votes, then three-fourths of the states must approve.[166] The machinery of the Constitution is precisely calibrated to discourage a change like this.

We came close in recent memory. The 1968 election scared many from both parties, because racist independent candidate George Wallace came close to denying an Electoral College victory to the winner—and could have bargained for the presidency with civil rights laws as a chip. In 1969, the House overwhelmingly voted to end the Electoral College system. Both LBJ and Richard Nixon supported the move. Only seventy lawmakers voted no. But the measure was filibustered to death in the Senate by senators from low-turnout, mostly southern, states, who worried their interests would be overwhelmed by urban voting blocs. Then a few years later, a similar plan was stymied by new opposition from African Americans and Jews, concentrated in large states, who worried that the current system forces candidates to pay attention to them. Logically, it's hard for both arguments to be right. Even if Congress were to pass such a measure, it would then face hurdles in the states. States with small congressional delegations would fear losing power, even as more people gained clout, in a popular vote.

Since it's so hard to pass an amendment, people have searched for creative ways to fix things without changing the Constitution.

A Bad Idea: District-by-District Voting

Nearly everywhere, the winner takes all the state's electoral votes. Democrats are especially strong in California, and thus its fifty-five electoral votes are key to their election bloc. In 2007, a petition drive sought to put the "Presidential Election Reform Act" on the California ballot as an initiative. Under its terms, the winner in each congressional district gets that district's electoral vote. It sounds reasonable at first, but on closer look, the arguments for it crumble like a mummy hitting air.

Most simply, to take this step in only one big state would simply siphon off votes from one party, in this case the Democrats. (Hence the GOP lawyers behind the effort.) Columnist Bob Herbert estimates that twenty electoral votes would have gone to Bush that went to Kerry in 2004. To make this change in only one state guarantees a partisan tilt. (North Carolina

Democrats were poised to try something similar, but national leaders yanked them back.)

A district-by-district vote would put the entire presidential poll at the mercy of creative gerrymandering. Only three of California's congressional districts are remotely competitive. *Newsweek's* Jonathan Alter notes, "And if the idea was somehow adopted nationally, it would mean competing for votes in only about 60 far-flung congressional districts—roughly seven percent of the country. Everyone else's vote would not 'count,' if you want to look at it that way."[167] The Federal Voting Rights Act also makes sure that district lines are drawn to give African Americans and other minorities a chance to be represented in Congress. But in a presidential race, the effect would be to dilute their vote by squeezing them into a handful of districts.

A BETTER IDEA: NATIONAL POPULAR VOTE

We can circumvent the Electoral College and create a popular vote, without a constitutional amendment. It's called National Popular Vote, and it takes a little explaining. The Constitution gives states the power over how to allocate electors. Each state is being asked to pass a law entering into a binding agreement to award all their electors to the candidate who wins the *national* popular vote in all fifty states and Washington, D.C. This provision goes into effect only when states whose electoral votes total a majority—currently, 270—sign the same compact. When that happens, whoever wins the popular vote will garner a majority of electoral votes. And while it is rather complex, it has the advantage of being fair, utterly nonpartisan and—if it works—rendering the Electoral College a charmingly archaic formality. Devised by a mathematician and two law professors, it is being pushed by the National Popular Vote campaign, the election reform organization FairVote, and a collection of former lawmakers of both parties.[168]

The proposal is fair (it's nationwide), it helps neither party, and it could go into effect right away. It would seem tailor-made for a post-partisan leader such as Arnold Schwarzenegger. Unfortunately, the California governor vetoed this measure in 2006. Maryland became the first state to sign the compact, followed by New Jersey and Illinois; other states are expected to follow suit.

Changing the Constitution through state laws may seem like a meandering path toward fundamental reform, but there's precedent in the move to direct election of senators. For most of the country's history, state legislators, not voters, chose U.S. senators. When Abraham Lincoln debated Stephen Douglas, citizens couldn't vote for them—they were voting for legislators who would then choose the man to send to Washington. The system was prone to corruption and a bulwark against popular will at the polls. In 1905, a muckraking magazine called *Cosmopolitan* (not that *Cosmo*) published a series, *The Treason of the Senate*. The Progressives began to agitate for direct election of senators, but then as now it was hard and slow to change the Constitution. So legislators ran for office pledging to vote for whoever won nonbinding "beauty contest" elections. By the time the Constitution actually was revised, many senators already were effectively elected by the voters. With National Popular Vote, the Electoral College may never need to be stricken from the Constitution. But for practical purposes, it would be rendered a formality, a charming relic of a time when lawmakers took snuff and democracy was the furthest thing from politicians' minds.

* * *

By reforming elections we would likely alter the way campaigns are run and hence the way policies are formed. These changes do not embrace other, arguably more innovative (and certainly more unorthodox) systems for assessing the popular will, such as proportional representation or instant runoff voting, which lets voters indicate their second choice in elections. They do not pivot to direct democracy, such as the proposals for voter-driven initiative and referenda that marked reform efforts decades ago, and which have had mixed results in states such as California. The changes in this chapter, instead, take as a given the basic mechanics of American democracy: representative government, with the candidate who gets the most votes winning, drawn from the major parties. If nothing else, it is politically easier to imagine public understanding of these changes.

And if we get politics right, it would make a huge difference, in forcing public officials to represent a much broader segment of the populace out of electoral self-interest. Combined with reforms in the voting system, these changes could have massive impact on American life.

But even if we fix voting and reform politics, there is more to do. The core self-regulating system of American government—checks and balances—is badly out of joint. The presidency has assumed greater power, while Congress has receded from its strong role. Professional agencies have become grossly politicized. To renew democracy, we need to repair government. That is the subject of the next chapter.

REPAIRING GOVERNMENT

PART THREE: REPAIRING GOVERNMENT

"Conscience is the inner voice that warns us somebody may be looking."—H. L. Mencken

A strong presidency is critical to America. "Energy in the executive," as Alexander Hamilton put it, remains a driving force for policymaking, and has often been the principal source for progressive governance. In times of crisis, it is certainly understandable that power flows to the commander in chief. We expect presidents to play a lead role in conducting foreign policy and in protecting our security. The benefits of a strong presidency go beyond that. Only a president—who speaks with one voice, in contrast to the cacophony of 535 members of Congress—can articulate national vision and frame issues to overcome the system's built-in tendency toward stasis. It was FDR who pushed an isolationist country to prepare for World War II. It was Lyndon Johnson—backing the civil rights movement—who moved voting rights through Congress. It was Ronald Reagan who pushed through tax and budget policies that shrank the federal government and deregulated the economy. Liberals don't like it when George W. Bush pushes deregulatory policies. But they didn't mind when Bill Clinton issued a flurry of executive orders protecting the environment. Such "presidential administration" can be necessary to wriggle free from the clench of divided government.[169] "Where you stand depends upon where you sit" is not a compelling theory of executive power.

But the past six years have seen not a strong presidency, but a dangerous one. The abuses go far, far beyond the acceptable levels of energetic policymaking expected of a president in demanding times. Constitutional order depends upon the fealty of those in power, a willingness to follow the rules and "color within the lines," even if inconvenient or frustrating. A strong presidency can flourish only within the rule of law and the Constitution. But President Bush has crashed through those boundaries at such breakneck speed that he likely will weaken the presidency going forward. Many people now hear defense of a strong executive as support for torture or disregard for even elementary checks and balances. That's appalling.

Checks and balances are the signal contribution of American democracy to the world. As Eric Lane and Michael Oreskes note in their book *The Genius of America,* unlike others before and since, the Founders did not try to create a government to reflect some idealized notion of humanity, or to force the spring of a "New Man."[170] Rather, they assumed people would act in self-interest, and set those forces against one another to assure accountability. "Ambition must be made to counteract ambition," explained James Madison in *The Federalist.* Checks and balances are the way our system assures that one person or group does not overwhelm the views of others, at least not permanently. Such accountability mechanisms make it less likely that bad policies will be heedlessly pursued, especially in foreign policy. Democracies, not just autocracies, go to war, but they are less likely to wage them illegitimately or foolishly.[171] When checks and balances work they give effective voice to the citizenry, who have multiple channels to express praise or opposition to policy.

The damage done to public institutions in recent years will take years to fix. As is well known, the current administration outdid its predecessors by its doctrinally fierce effort to expand presidential power. As significant, and more unusual, Congress sharply receded from its longstanding role as originator of policy and oversight. The legislative branch became harshly partisan, its members seeing themselves as party standard-bearers more than as leaders of an independent branch with distinct duties. At times, Congress nearly ground to a halt as an effective and independent institution. And repair is needed, as well, in the great expert agencies of the government, especially the Justice Department, where professionalism has been overwhelmed by politics.

The current mess goes beyond party, and it's not enough to trust the goodwill of the people we elect. So our democracy movement must insist on new laws to repair the checks and balances and thus restore the basic structure of American government.

7

RESTORE CHECKS AND BALANCES

Replacing Nixon and Cheney with Madison and Hamilton

In 1975, Richard Nixon told interviewer David Frost, "When the president does it, that means that it is not illegal." Nixon's statement, so extreme that he dared not utter it until after he left office, caused a furor. A decade later, a congressional committee probed the Iran Contra scandal, in which the White House had sold arms to Iran and used the proceeds to buy arms for rebels in Nicaragua—all despite laws to the contrary. The committee's minority report echoed Nixon's view. It argued that "the Chief Executive will on occasion feel duty bound to assert monarchical notions of prerogative that will permit him to exceed the laws."[172] The lead lawmaker authoring that report was a young congressman, Dick Cheney of Wyoming. Two decades later, reporters on Air Force Two asked Cheney to justify the administration's decision to launch a domestic spying program without telling Congress or getting court approval. If you want to know his views, Cheney urged the journalists, take a look at the Minority

Report. "[O]ver the years there had been an erosion of presidential power and authority," he explained. "The president of the United States needs to have his constitutional powers unimpaired, if you will, in terms of the conduct of national security policy."[173]

Repeatedly, leaders insist, "Everything changed on September 11th." But this theory of untrammeled presidential power was not a product of 9/11. It was a bad idea whose time had come.

In crisis and war, power invariably surges to the chief executive. Abraham Lincoln suspended habeas corpus during the Civil War. Franklin Roosevelt interned hundreds of thousands of Americans of Japanese ancestry. But these leaders acted openly and knew they had done something out of the ordinary, outside of the constitutional order, justifiable only (if that) by an immediate emergency threatening the country. Lincoln acted while Congress was out of session, and he announced that legislators must either approve what he had done or punish him.

By contrast, President George W. Bush has argued that he can act at will due to broad powers inherent in the presidency. All presidents want power, often the more the better. But few have been so focused on breaking down barriers to executive authority. Bush took to illogical extreme a theory developed by conservative professors and judges: the idea of the "unitary executive," in which the president claims all the authority of the executive branch in his hands. This theory can go as far as arguing that the president alone decides how to interpret the law governing his role—that Congress cannot tie the hands of government agencies or create independent agencies. Applied indiscriminately, this theory can be used to define away nearly any restrictions on presidential fiat. Fritz Schwarz and Aziz Huq point out in their book *Unchecked and Unbalanced,* "Unlike Lincoln and other past chief executives, President Bush asserts that he has the power to set aside fundamental laws permanently—including those that ban torture and domestic spying."[174]

More, through history most abuses occurred in full public view. President Bush has insisted that his assertions of executive authority be kept secret. The public later learned that a series of memorandums by lawyers at the Justice Department authorized the use of torture, kidnapping, and other extraordinary steps, memos that still mostly have been kept secret. Conservative law professor Jack Goldsmith learned of these legal opinions when he became the head of the Office of Legal Counsel, the elite office that opines on constitutional law for the leaders of the government. He withdrew them, he wrote, because they were "sloppily reasoned, overbroad, and incautious in asserting extraordinary constitutional authorities on behalf of the president."[175] (Later, secretly, they were reinstituted in a modified form.)

Bush's theory of an unchecked executive was given its most brazen public expression in a series of remarkable signing statements issued by the White House to explain what the president means when he signs a bill into law. For the first six years of his presidency, George W. Bush did not veto a single measure passed by Congress. Routinely he would sign new laws, handing out souvenir pens and posing for pictures with lawmakers. Later, quietly, he would issue a "signing statement" announcing he would simply not be bound by parts of the laws he did not like—claiming the right to do so under his expanded view of constitutional power. Few noticed this pattern of presidential crossed-fingers until a Pulitzer Prize–winning *Boston Globe* series appeared in April 2006, reporting that Bush was refusing to enforce one in ten laws he had signed.[176]

The American Bar Association found that President Bush issued 800 signing statements challenging bills he signed, significantly more than all previous presidents put together.[177] For example, when Congress, after much debate, passed the amendment offered by John McCain forbidding officials from using torture or cruel, inhuman, or degrading treatment on prisoners, President Bush signed the measure but issued a statement saying he had the right to waive the requirement. Similarly, he signed a law requiring officials to report to Congress when they use Patriot Act authority to secretly search homes and seize private papers; again, Bush simply issued a statement blithely noting that he refused to follow that law. The ABA Task Force called the signing statements "contrary to the rule of law and our constitutional system."

Many abuses flowed from this misguided theory of unbridled presidential power. As we now know, the U.S. government conducted widespread torture of prisoners. It greatly expanded the practice of "extraordinary rendition," in which our government kidnaps terrorism suspects and spirits them off to other countries, where they will likely be tortured. It undertook a program of electronic surveillance of U.S. citizens without a warrant from a special court, as required by law. Had the administration asked the court for such a warrant, it would likely have been issued. Congress could have passed a law to authorize the monitoring, but the administration appeared to prefer to act without Congress or the court, just to show that it could. It was more important that it be done illegally than that it be done legally.

Such misuse of power in the Bush presidency is now widely understood and decried. *But it continues.* For the first six years of the administration, Congress conducted virtually no oversight of the executive branch. Since the Democrats won the Congress in 2006, oversight hearings have returned, a significant improvement. But they have tended to focus more on domestic concerns than on vital national security questions. And substantive restrictions on the prerogatives of the executive branch have failed to materialize. A combination of party discipline among minority Republicans, irresolution by majority Democrats, and paralyzing fear of being branded "soft on terrorism" have left Congress frozen.

Fixing Congress, the "Broken Branch"

The unbridled executive power of the Bush–Cheney years by now is familiar. Less understood, and possibly as disturbing in the long run, is the decline of Congress.

During the early years of the Cold War, Congress fell into the habit of deferring to presidents on foreign policy (though never on domestic policy). For the last three decades of the twentieth century, though, Congress asserted its authority. It created a budget process that strengthened lawmakers' broad ability to set spending and tax totals, created the highly respected Congressional Budget Office, and set up intelligence committees to ensure that lawmakers were told of key national security moves. The long-abused power of committee barons, which helped block civil rights laws for decades, was replaced with a more transparent system that gave new power both to congressional leaders and to rank-and-file lawmakers. This system opened more opportunities for special-interest influence than before, since there were more decision makers to influence, but also provided a more inclusive and open policy process.

Over the past decade, though, the basic institutions of Congress broke down. Thomas Mann and Norman Ornstein are prominent political scientists. Neither is known as a partisan—both are prominent members of the capital's establishment. In 2006 they studied Congress and concluded that its institutions were badly broken. "In 37 years each of Congress-watching, we have never seen the institution in worse shape," they wrote.[178]

The decline of conference committees, the little-known forum where the most intense legislative bargaining took place for a century, is one example. A conference committee, drawn from both the House and Senate, is appointed when the chambers have passed different versions of the same legislation. The minutiae of legislation arise from these sessions. Sessions are public. Often, they were unedifying, as lawmakers huddled, aides whispered, and lobbyists passed notes and scrambled to catch the eye of a legislator. Still, they were open meetings, with the sessions transcribed for other lawmakers and the record. Even on critical legislation, the work was done through the conference committee. Imagine a vivid scene from days gone by: lawmakers working all night around a square table to hash out the numbing details of the savings and loan bailout. It was rarely linear, often messy, with aides whispering in lawmakers' ears, reporters squinting for a hint of compromise, and nervous lobbyists yearning to catch the eye of a powerful lawmaker to pass on a message with the wiggle of an eyebrow. It was untidy, but public. In the past decade, conference committees no longer mattered. They still met even when their original function had been long forgotten, like the Masons. Republican leaders stacked the committees and excluded Democrats. And all the real legislating was done through secret negotiations conducted by the leaders of the governing party.

Changes in party balance have helped restore some of Congress's role. But institutional change is needed for the long run.

RESTORE HABEAS CORPUS

A key check on executive power was first crafted in a tent at Runnymede in the south of England in the year 1215. There the barons of England confronted King John and forced him to sign the Magna Carta, committing to the rule of law and limiting the power of the monarch. At the heart was the writ of habeas corpus, which prohibits the executive from holding someone prisoner without giving him a chance to find out why he is being held and to prove his innocence. (*Habeas corpus* means "produce the body" in Latin.)[179]

Our own Declaration of Independence objected to King George III's abuse of his detention power. In *The Federalist,* Alexander Hamilton declared habeas corpus a "bulwark" of individual liberty, calling secret imprisonment the most "dangerous engine of arbitrary government."[180] When the Framers drafted the Constitution, they debated not whether to include habeas corpus, but in what rare instances it could ever be suspended. The Constitution says starkly, "The privilege of the Writ of Habeas Corpus shall not be suspended, unless when in Cases of Rebellion or Invasion the public Safety may require it," and only by act of Congress.[181] Throughout the years, prisoners had the right to file habeas corpus petitions before a federal court to challenge their confinement. It has been suspended only for brief times and in specific locations, such as in some communities in the South after the Civil War, when courts could not function.

In pursuing the "Global War on Terror," however, the Bush administration has insisted on its right to hold hundreds, perhaps thousands of individuals without trial. Federal courts repeatedly have ruled Bush's policy unconstitutional. Several Supreme Court cases have held that courts have the right to intervene, and that individuals can challenge their detention. Justice Sandra Day O'Connor wrote for the court in *Hamdi v. Rumsfeld,* "We have long since made clear that a state of war is not a blank check for the President when it comes to the rights of the Nation's citizens."[182]

Faced with a string of commands from the justices to provide basic rights to detainees, the Bush administration persuaded Congress to strip away those rights through two newly enacted laws. The Military Commissions Act, passed in 2005, and the Detainee Treatment Act, passed in 2006, are dark landmarks in American law. They suspend habeas corpus permanently, not just for a limited period of time. They suspend it for a whole class of people, too—anyone the president of the moment declares to be an "enemy combatant." It is not limited to al Qaeda or today's struggle against terrorism. It's all up to the president. No finding of a national security threat is required, either. President Bush has asserted that the "Global War" is of indefinite duration. The suspension of habeas corpus and detention without trial is expected to be indefinite, too.

How did these provisions become law? The main purpose of the law Congress passed in 2006 was to make clear that torture was illegal. Only at the last minute did the White House insist on the provision stripping habeas corpus, which ironically made it nearly impossible for anyone who had been tortured to do anything about it. Senator Arlen Specter, then the chairman of the Judiciary Committee, urged the Senate to remove the language, but the effort fell short by two votes. Now, with a new Congress, Specter has teamed up with the Democrat who succeeded him as chairman of the panel, Patrick Leahy of Vermont. Their measure would restore habeas corpus for those detained by the United States. It faces a certain veto from President Bush, though many who are running to succeed him have endorsed it.

That this measure is necessary is a sign of how our democratic institutions have slipped. At stake, of course, is principle: the right to habeas corpus now has been denied to only a relatively small number of prisoners, some of whom are innocent but some of whom undoubtedly have been up to no good. But this president's insistence that he can lock up residents of the United States indefinitely as "enemy combatants," if allowed to stand, could be used against many more Americans and foreigners in coming years. By placing the power to detain indefinitely in the hands of one man or woman, without judicial scrutiny, we are handing to the executive a level of command that through history has been prone to abuse. If there is another, more serious terrorist attack on a U.S. city, for example, we can imagine a future president seizing many more "suspects."

There's a more immediate impact when we fail to live up to our own democratic values. In his leaked 2003 memo, then Secretary of Defense Donald Rumsfeld asked a pointed question that should guide future counterterrorism policy:

Are we capturing, killing or deterring and dissuading more terrorists every day than the madrassas and the radical clerics are recruiting, training and deploying against us?[183]

The sense that the United States is a country that honors the rule of law and basic human rights has long been one of our greatest foreign-policy assets. But in the global struggle against al Qaeda and its affiliates, the idea that the United States no longer plays by its own rules is a huge recruiting boon to our enemies. Allegations of torture and images from the military prison at Abu Ghraib have led to a state in which, as former Secretary of State Colin Powell said, "The world is beginning to doubt the moral basis of our fight against terrorism."[184] Donald Rumsfeld's successor, Robert Gates, warned that the treatment of those detained at Guantanamo "taints" the fight against terrorism and deprives this country of international credibility.[185] (Gates urged that the Guantanamo facility simply be closed.) Disregarding longstanding constitutional protections simply offers new ammunition to those who assert the United States is a lawless hyperpower.

Restoring habeas corpus involves several steps. Congress must repeal those sections of the earlier laws that ended habeas corpus. Beyond that, the nation should legislate to bring our global detention system under the rule of law. And we should end the practice of extralegal transfers of prisoners to countries that we know engage in torture, even when those countries insist they won't torture these prisoners.[186]

PUTTING TEETH IN OVERSIGHT

In the past, regardless of which party controlled the White House or the Congress, lawmakers used congressional committees to conduct oversight of the activities of the executive branch. Senator Harry S Truman made his name by probing government contracting under the Roosevelt administration. The Senate Foreign Relations Committee held hearings, broadcast live on national television, exploring the Vietnam War. The "Church Committee" (named after its chair, Frank Church) revealed abuses of presidential power by Democratic and Republican White Houses. In the early 1990s, Congress probed both policy failures and scandals of the Democratic administration, even though the Congress was controlled by the same party. (For example, the first extensive hearings on the Whitewater controversy were held by Democratic-controlled committees in 1994.)

Oversight began to break down in the late 1990s. The newly Republican-controlled Congress zealously probed dozens of scandals, real or imagined. (The House took 140 hours of sworn testimony on the use of the White House Christmas card list.[187]) Substantive oversight lagged well behind.

Then, when George W. Bush won the White House and one party assumed control over both elected branches of government, oversight simply vanished. The Center for American Progress catalogued a partial list of the topics that *didn't* get oversight during the first six years of Bush's presidency: "The failure of pre–Iraq war intelligence on weapons of mass destruction; the failure to conclude the so called 'Phase II' of the Senate investigation regarding political manipulation of intelligence; the refusal to investigate allegations of torture and ill-treatment of detainees; the failure to obtain a proper understanding of, let alone robust oversight over, the NSA warrantless program; and the failure to pass the Intelligence Authorization Act for the first time in nearly 30 years."[188]

A single House committee deluged the Clinton administration with over 1,000 subpoenas.[189] "In stark contrast," as journalist Ronald Brownstein notes, "no congressional committee ever subpoenaed the White House while the Republicans controlled the House for the first six years of Bush's presidency, and the Senate for all but about eighteen months during that period." During this time the White House received precisely one subpoena.[190]

Now, after the 2006 election, Congress changed hands—hasn't that jolted oversight to life? To some degree, it has. Rep. Henry Waxman, for example, chairs the Committee on Oversight and Government Affairs, and has skillfully exposed the use of private security forces in Iraq such as Blackwater, potentially improper use of government resources for campaign purposes, and political pressure on the Surgeon General, to name a few. The Judiciary Committees of both chambers did significant work to expose the U.S. attorney firings. But other than those highlights, many committees have been slow to use oversight as a tool not just for exposing scandal but for building policy arguments.

We must find ways to institutionalize oversight, to assure that Congress will play its counterbalancing role regardless of who is president and what level of political willpower exists.

In fact, there are deep structural reasons for the drop-off in oversight. When the Framers created the system of checks and balances, political parties had not yet formed. Indeed, such "factions" were considered abhorrent; George Washington's Farewell Address warned against them.[191] For most of the country's history, members of Congress jealously guarded their institutional role. Through these years, parties were disparate coalitions. Democrats included southern conservatives (who dominated Congress) and northern liberals. Republicans fused Wall Street–backed moderates and Main Street, small-town conservatives. Then two trends converged. First, the parties became more ideological, like European parties, especially after Ronald Reagan transformed the GOP into a bastion of movement conservatism. Southern conservative whites—long used to voting Republican for president but not yet Congress—moved fully into the party of Lincoln. Northern moderate Republicans (once known as "gypsy moths") vanished or switched to the Democrats. Second, at the same time, voters began to choose divided government, routinely electing a president of one party and a Congress of another. Voters have given control of both branches to one party in fewer than seven of the past twenty-six years.[192] The Republicans' refusal to conduct basic oversight was novel, and unlike the country's past. Given party alignment, though, it may augur the future.

Professors Rick Pildes and Daryl Levinson have proposed a change in the way Congress works that reflects the reality that the checks and balances come between parties as much as between branches.[193] Government divided among sharply differing parties now appears to be the norm. Tools for minority parties are blunt. The filibuster—the threat of an endless talkathon in the Senate—was used sparingly earlier. Now, in effect, a supermajority of sixty votes is needed for anything of significance.[194] But the heart of congressional oversight comes not on the Senate floor, but in committee rooms. In Germany and other countries whose constitutions were built after the experience of totalitarianism, minority parties are guaranteed rights, including setting legislative agenda and a share of witnesses before committees. In the United States, by contrast, only the majority generally can call hearings, summon witnesses, and control the calendar of committees. Majority status always will and should mean greater power. But too often minority status today means effectively *no* power to conduct oversight. Pildes and Levinson propose that members of the minority party be given the power to call witnesses or launch committee investigations. For example, a rule could require the minority party be given one-third of the witnesses at any hearing called by a congressional committee. More significant, rules could require that a certain number of hearings be called every year solely at the behest of the minority. The minority should have the ability, when necessary, to require documents—perhaps even issue subpoenas. At the very least, this would ensure that necessary documents and testimony can be squeezed out of the executive branch when Congress and the presidency are marching in lockstep.

The Department of Justice Purge

Politics has come to pervade government agencies long regarded as properly independent and driven by expertise. Climate change science was rewritten under the instructions of junior White House political aides. The Surgeon General was ordered to mention the president's name three times on every page of a speech.[195] The contracting process, long insulated from favoritism, routinely steered massive contracts to politically favored firms (for example, the huge contracts to Halliburton or the private military firm Blackwater for work in Iraq).[196]

At the Justice Department, political considerations were so deeply injected into law enforcement they led to the resignation of the Attorney General and his top aides, the most severe justice scandal since Watergate.

In 2002, Attorney General John Ashcroft made "ballot integrity" a top Justice Department priority.[197] A cadre of voter fraud commissars moved into the Civil Rights division. One young lawyer, Bradley Schlozman, became acting head of the voting unit, where he took to hiring and firing with the zest of a ward heeler. He reassigned four minority women, he told one colleague, to "make room for some good Americans."[198] Half the hires for career jobs—that is, civil service—belonged to conservative legal groups.[199] As political cronies crammed in, career lawyers were squeezed out. Since

2005 at least half the professional lawyers in the voting rights section left the division or quit the Justice Department altogether.[200] Schlozman's colleague Hans von Spakovsky anonymously wrote a law review article praising his own work.[201]

The hunt for "voter fraud" reached manic intensity in the run-up to the 2006 election. Karl Rove warned a gathering of Republicans lawyers, "We are, in some parts of the country, I am afraid to say, beginning to look like we have elections like those run in countries where the guys in charge are, you know, colonels in mirrored sunglasses."[202] He listed key battleground states where he thought fraud was at play. President Bush complained to Attorney General Alberto Gonzales that members of Congress were complaining of lax voter fraud prosecutions.[203] Prosecutors faced enormous pressure to bring charges against voter fraud by black and Latino voters—and if they refused, it turned out, they risked being put on a list for firing. Under a new, nearly unknown part of the U.S.A. Patriot Act, the Attorney General could now name U.S. attorneys without the Senate assent that had been required for two centuries.

Months before the 2006 election, the U.S. attorney for the Western District of Missouri was asked to resign, at least in part because he did not bring enough voter fraud prosecutions.[204] Bradley Schlozman moved in as "interim" U.S. attorney amid a tightly fought U.S.

Senate race. On November 1, he announced indictments of voter registration workers in a press release so rushed it got the names wrong.[205] "This national investigation is very much ongoing," he added vaguely. Because such charges so close to an election are inevitably explosive, the Justice Department had clear internal rules warning prosecutors not to bring them.[206] Later, under oath, Schlozman insisted he brought the Election Week indictments "at the direction" of an official at the home office. Then a few days later, he "clarified" his testimony, admitting he had decided to bring the indictment himself.[207]

Other U.S. attorneys were fired because of their failure to prosecute supposed voter fraud. David Iglesias of New Mexico, a clean-cut former military lawyer, was a model for the character played by Tom Cruise in *A Few Good Men*. Iglesias investigated 100 voter fraud cases, and concluded there was no basis for bringing charges in 99 of them, and that the one case with merit lacked the evidence for a courtroom win. Days before the election, Sen. Pete Domenici called him angrily, demanding indictments against Democrats. "The senator wanted to know whether I was going to file corruption charges …before November," Iglesias later recalled. "When I told him that I didn't think so, he said, 'I am very sorry to hear that,' and the line went dead."[208] Domenici then called the White House to demand that Iglesias be fired. The head of the New

Mexico Republican Party, furious that voter fraud prosecutions hadn't happened, accosted Karl Rove at a Christmas party, demanding, "Is anything ever going to happen to that guy?" Rove reassured him: "He's gone."[209]

Iglesias was joined on the purge list by John McKay, the prosecutor in Washington State. In 2004, a Democrat won the governorship after a recount. Republican leaders demanded that McKay bring voter fraud charges, but when he investigated, he found no reason to prosecute. Months later, McKay recalled, White House Counsel Harriet Miers "asked me why Republicans in the state of Washington would be angry with me."[210] She blocked his promotion to a judgeship. Then his name was added to the dismissal list.

One after another, the attorneys who refused to bring political prosecutions found themselves marked for firing. The *Washington Post* later conducted a body count:

> *Of the 12 U.S. attorneys known to have been dismissed or considered for removal [in 2006], five were identified by Rove or other administration officials as working in districts that were trouble spots for voter fraud—Kansas City, Mo.; Milwaukee; New Mexico; Nevada; and Washington state. Four of the five prosecutors in those districts were dismissed.*[211]

It is a sign of how atrophied the accountability muscles had become that the purge happened after the congressional election, when the Congress—and its subpoena power—was newly in the hands of the opposition party. David Iglesias broke silence and told the story of the political pressure he faced, soon joined by the other former prosecutors. After months of hearings, a central mystery remained: who drew up the list of attorneys to be fired? Many observers assumed Karl Rove. The White House admitted that thousands of key emails were routed through a nongovernmental computer system, seemingly in an effort to keep the messages from being preserved as required by federal law. President Bush's lawyers refused to let Rove answer questions in a flurry of claims of executive privilege. In painful appearances before congressional committees, Attorney General Albert Gonzales could not recall when he fired the attorneys, or why, but he was sure he had done so and that it was the right thing to do. By August 2007, Gonzales, his deputy, and his chief of staff had resigned.

THE DEMOCRACY MOMENT

PART FOUR: THE DEMOCRACY MOMENT

"As our case is new, so we must think anew, and act anew. We must disenthrall ourselves, and then we shall save our country."—Abraham Lincoln

All through American history, pressure for change builds, often unseen, until suddenly it is time, once again, for renewal. A wide sense that institutions do not work collides with the unorganized but potent energy of a broad mass of citizens. The range of the possible widens. We are in such a moment now, with plunging approval ratings and soaring Internet activism only two ingredients for political ferment. This combination—of felt need and public engagement—comes only fleetingly. We must use this democracy moment to insist on transformative change. During this election season, we must insist that candidates share their plans for renewing democracy as readily as they share their plans for health care, taxes, or climate change. It is now—when the problems with our elections are laid bare—that political leaders can be forced to commit to reforming public institutions.

Some of the changes described in this book can happen immediately, before the election. For example, backup paper ballots can and should be made available in polling places with electronic machines. Voters should insist that election officials in every state make sure that there are as many voting machines in poor neighborhoods as there are in leafy suburbs. In light of battles over voter ID and other possibly disenfranchising measures that will rage through 2008 and up until minutes before the election, we should insist on a moratorium on any new laws that would raise the barriers to voting before Election Day.

But far more significant than 2008, is 2009. A new administration and new Congress will have a window of a few short months during which they can begin to make the most fundamental changes before budget deadlines press, and unexpected foreign crises crowd in. It's critical to take advantage of the momentum offered a new administration. The new president and Congress should consider moving quickly, in the first weeks, to pass strong democracy reforms. In 1993, President Clinton pressed his budget plan and then health care, only to run into the wall of public antipathy toward government. Many strategists, including at times Clinton himself, concluded that it would have been wiser for him to focus on campaign finance, lobbying disclosure, and changes in government programs such as welfare first. That would have signaled to a wary public that the new administration would first tame the capital before giving it new power. Even more important, such action would have scrambled the traditional power relationships among interest groups and their patrons in Congress enough that they would not be able to regroup in time to stop other reforms down the road—in effect sweeping aside the pieces on the chess board—to best see the first move.

The politics of democracy renewal are messy. Many reforms fall uneasily on a spectrum of "right" and "left." They stir uncomfortable issues of race and class. Because such reforms often are most sought by unorganized citizens, it is easy for political leaders to spurn change or simply be distracted by more tightly organized, well-funded communities. But we can achieve these changes—and so prepare America for the next 230 years of her life.

We have done it before. A century ago, in the Progressive era, churning social and economic change created new opportunity and broad economic growth, but spawned new inequality and economic and status insecurity. Existing governmental institutions came to be widely viewed as corrupt, inefficient, and not up to the task of managing a modern nation. The response did not seek to overturn the American order (as did, say, European socialism). It was not explicitly class based, either, as the earlier Populist movement had been. Instead it reflected the intense and creative political energy of a new and largely nonideological middle class and professionalized business leadership. And, also important, it focused on the *how* of politics as much as the *what*. Bold political leaders such as Theodore Roosevelt, Woodrow Wilson, and dozens of mayors and legislators worked with networks of journalists and public interest groups to win change. Some of the reforms were half-measures, and some did not last. But many did. From modern workplace health and safety regulation, to the creation of the Federal Reserve, to core democracy reforms such as direct elections of senators and extension of the vote to women, the Progressives breathed new life into American democracy—and opened the way to a new century of progress.

As happened a century ago, such a movement can become a governing ethos that drives a hopeful time in our history.

★ ★ ★

But will these reforms matter? Will an influx, say, of new voters or a turn toward publicly financed campaigns really change things? Of course, it is hard to know for sure. But there is strong reason to think that making these seven bold changes would change America.

At a bare minimum, more participation will open the political system to a wider and more diverse electorate. Those who do not vote tend to be poorer, less educated, and more harried than those who do. (Certainly the moves to disenfranchise voters target minorities, the elderly, and young citizens.) Nonvoters don't share unified views on issues—for example, many may be socially more conservative while economically more populist than a typical suburban electorate. But there can be no doubt that a working political system forced to be responsive to a far more expansive group of voters may produce different policies. In any event, the political system and the government it produces will be seen as far more legitimate.

If we can free lawmakers from the demented demands of fundraising we will liberate policymaking as well. Elected officials would be able to devote far more attention to their "day job" of serving the taxpayer. Beyond that, the overwhelming power of entrenched economic interests to block change within their own bailiwick will continue to be the most fundamental obstacle to policy change. Our pluralist democracy gains from the amplified voices of many interests. But in recent decades, campaign money combined with lobbying and the revolving door has led not to creative cacophony but paralysis. Sweeping political reform can upset the calculus. Imagine the impact on energy policy, say, if the oil industry no longer serves as a major source of campaign cash for (or against) lawmakers. Consider, too, how hard it will be to pass meaningful health care reform without political reform. Health reform wins cheers on the campaign trail. But the health insurance and pharmaceutical industries, as well as doctors and other economic groups, are far louder in the halls of Congress. A new chief executive may claim a broad public mandate. But nearly all members of Congress will have run ahead of the president in their own district. And the lobbyists and the industries they represent are a more reliable source of campaign funding and political organization. Unorganized citizens will fare poorly against organized money, unless there is galvanizing institutional change.

Ultimately, these democracy reforms can achieve better policy and a more effective government. Checks and balances—both between the branches and between the government and the public—are not just a means to curb unwise power. They are vital mechanisms for self-correction, critical ways to detect and deter error.

Much as the problems intertwine, the solutions reinforce. Increasing competition in elections, for example, leads to higher turnout. (As political scientist Michael McDonald notes, "All but hardcore sports fans tune out a blowout."[212])

If we take these steps, we will be writing our own chapter in the long story of American democracy—a story that echoes far beyond our borders. The health of American democracy at home and the strength of American policy abroad long have reinforced. A renewed America can once again serve as a beacon to the world. Lincoln understood this: he signed the Emancipation Proclamation in part to stop England from recognizing the Confederacy. Roosevelt's Four Freedoms were premised on the positive example of revived American democracy. Eisenhower's Attorney General urged the Supreme Court to declare segregation unconstitutional because we simply could not credibly woo newly independent African nations if we did not stop practicing Jim Crow. Ronald Reagan cited the Pilgrims' notion of the New World as a "shining city on a hill" as a model of what can be, visible to all.

In 2006, I visited Istanbul to attend a gathering of human rights advocates from around the world. The hallways were thick with people from Central Asia, the former Soviet republics, and Africa. They were fighting for the same causes I was fighting for—democracy and the rule of law. They were dismayed by the turn our democracy had taken. They had looked to the United States as a model, an inspiration, a source of prestige for their work, and saw the work to *restore* American democracy as critical to their own efforts to *create* democracy.

Thomas Paine, in *Common Sense,* wrote words true then and truer today, "The cause of America is in a great measure the cause of all mankind." We can honor the spirit of our own founding, and make our nation again the cause of all humankind, if we once again put democracy at the center of our politics—where it belongs.

NOTES

1. For a broad history of democracy in America in the 19th Century, see the magisterial volume by Sean Wilentz, The Rise of American Democracy (New York: Norton, 2005). For a history of voting, see Alexander Keyssar, The Right to Vote: The Contested History of Democracy in the United States (New York: Basic Books, 2000).

2. See International Institute for Democracy and Electoral Assistance (IDEA) Voter Turnout Global Survey, available at http://www.idea.int/vt/survey/voter_turnout_pop2.cfm.

3. Bloomberg News columnist Al Hunt tallies the likely spending: "The current election cycle will look like this: The Republican and Democratic nominees combined will spend more than $1 billion by next November; other presidential hopefuls will fork over another $400 million; congressional candidates can be counted on to spend in excess of $1.5 billion, and the various Democratic and Republican party committees will part with more money than that. Throw in at least half a billion from 'independent' groups outside the campaigns and, bingo, you've topped $5 billion." Albert R. Hunt, "Letter from Washington: Candidates in race to spend," International Herald Tribune, November 25, 2007, available at http://www.iht.com/articles/2007/11/25/america/letter.php.

4. Jeffrey M. Jones, "Low Trust in Federal Government Rivals Watergate Era Levels," Gallup Poll, September 26, 2007, available at http://www.galluppoll.com/content/?ci=28795.

5. See James Surowiecki, The Wisdom of Crowds (New York: Doubleday, 2004).

6. Reynolds v. Sims, 377 U.S. 533 (1964).

7. See http://www.cnn.com/ELECTION/2000/results and http://www.cnn.com/ELECTION/2004.

8. Caltech/MIT Voting Technology Project Report, "CalTech/MIT Voting Technology Report: What Is; What Could Be" July 2001, page 8, available athttp://www.vote.caltech.edu/media/documents/july01/fast_facts.pdf.

9. Public Law 107–252.

10. U.S. Census, "Voting and Registration in the Election of 2004," available at http://www.census.gov/prod/2006pubs/p20556.pdf.

11. See, for example, Thomas Patterson, The Vanishing Voter: Public Involvement in an Age of Uncertainty (New York: Random House, 2003); Robert Putnam, Bowling Alone: The Collapse and Revival of American Community (New York: Simon and Schuster, 2001).

12. See U.S. Census Bureau, "Voting and Registration in the Election of November 2004," March 2006, 4–5. Available at http://www.census.gov/prod/2006pubs/p20-556.pdf

13. National Election Commission, Report of the Task Force on the Federal Election System, chapter 2, "Voter Registration," August 2001, available at http://www.tcf.org/Publications/ElectionReform/99_full_report.pdf.

14. Keyssar, The Right to Vote, p. 3.

15. The radicalism of the amendment's authors should be recalled when those opposed to civil rights cite "original intent" of the Framers to oppose a broad reading of the Constitution. See Nathan Newman and J. J. Gass, A New Birth of Freedom: The

Forgotten History of the 13th, 14th, and 15th Amendments (Brennan Center for Justice, 2004), available at http://www.brennancenter.org/dynamic/subpages/ji5.pdf.

16. See Eric Foner, Reconstruction: America's Unfinished Revolution, 1863–1877 (New York: Harper & Row, 1988), 354–355.

17. For a compelling recent discussion of the rolling back of black rights in the South, see Nicholas Lemann, Redemption: The Last Battle of the Civil War (New York: Farrar, Straus & Giroux, 2006).

18. C. Vann Woodward, The Strange Career of Jim Crow (New York: Oxford University Press, Commemorative Edition, 2001), 85.

19. Keyssar, The Right to Vote, p. 122.

20. Thomas Patterson, The Vanishing Voter: Public Involvement in an Age of Uncertainty (New York: Knopf, 2002), 178.

21. Demos, Project Vote, ACORN, "Ten Years Later: A Promise Unfulfilled," July 2005, available at http://projectvote.org/fileadmin/ProjectVote/pdfs/1Executive_Summary_of_Ten_Years_Later_A_Promise_Unfulfilled1.pdf.

22. Steven Hill, 10 Steps to Repair American Democracy (Sausalito, CA: PoliPoint Press, 2005), p. 37.

23. In 2000, only 47 percent of the voting-age population came to the polls in the United States. In Canada in the same year, 55 percent of adults went to the polls. See Institute for Democracy and Electoral Assistance (IDEA), "Voter Turnout: A Global Survey," at http://www.idea.int/vt/survey/index.cfm.

24. Wendy Weiser and Renee Paradis, Universal Voter Registration (Brennan Center for Justice, forthcoming).

25. Buckley v. American Constitutional Law Foundation, 525 U.S. 182, 195 (1999).

26. New America Foundation, "Universal Voter Registration: A Way to Empower and Engage All Californians," available at http://www.newamerica.net/files/Universal%20Voter%20Registration.pdf.

27. R. Michael Alvarez and Stephen Ansolabehere, California Votes, The Promise of Election Day Registration, 12, available at http://www.vote.caltech.edu/media/documents/wps/vtp_wp5.pdf. Other studies put the numbers even higher, although they don't take other factors into consideration. In 2004, Professor Mary Sullivan reported to the American Political Science Association that nearly three quarters of eligible voters in EDR states went to the polls, nearly 14 percent more than other states. See Mary Sullivan, "The Triggering Effects of Election Day Registration on Partisan Mobilization Activities in U.S. Elections," paper prepared for presentation at the Annual Meeting of the American Political Science Association, Washington, D.C., August 31–September 3, 2005, available at http://convention2.allacademic.com/getfile.php?file_apsa05_proceeding/2005–08–29/41525/apsa05_proceeding_41525.pdf.

28. See Lorraine Minnite, "Election Day Registration: A Study of Voter Fraud Allegations and Findings on Voter Roll Security," Demos (2004), available at http://www.demos.org/pubs/edr_fraud_web.pdf.

29. Micah Sifry, Minnesota Maverick, Salon.com, 10/30/98. http://www.salon.com/news/1998/10/30newsa.html

30. Steven Schier, "Jesse's Victory: It Was No Fluke," Washington Monthly, Jan./Feb. 1999, available at http://www.washingtonmonthly.com/features/1999/9901.schier.ventura.html.

31. See Henry F. Graff, Grover Cleveland (The American Presidents Series) (New York: Times Books, 2002), 65.

32. Jeff Manza and Christopher Uggen, Locked Out: Felon Disenfranchisement and American Democracy (New York: Oxford University Press, 2006), 248–250.

33. William J. Clinton, remarks at Common Cause "I Love an Ethical NY" dinner, November 1, 2005.

34. Ryan S. King and Mark Mauer, Distorted Priorities: Drug Offenders in State Prisons 1, 2002, available at http://www.soros.org/initiatives/justice/articles_publications/publications/distorted_20020901/9038.pdf.

35. Jeff Manza and Christopher Uggen, Locked Out: Felon Disenfranchisement and American Democracy (New York: Oxford University Press, 2006), Fig.4.1, 97

36. Erika L. Wood and Neema Trivedi, "The Modern Day Poll Tax: How Economic Sanctions Block Access to the Polls," Clearinghouse REVIEW Journal of Poverty Law and Policy, May–June 2007.

37. Manza and Uggen, Locked Out, p. 42.

38. President George W. Bush, Address on the State of the Union, January 20, 2004, available at http://www.whitehouse.gov/news/releases/2004/01/20040120–7.html.

39. Mary Ellen Klas and Gary Fineout, "Felon Rights on Faster Track," Miami Herald, April 28, 2007, available at http://www.miamiherald.com/458/story/174219.html.

40. R. Michael Alvarez, "Voter Registration: Past, Present and Future," Written Testimony Prepared for the Commission on Federal Election Reform, Caltech/MIT Voting Technology Project, June 17, 2005, available at http://american.edu/ia/cfer/0630test/alvarez.pdf.

41. Michael Powell and Peter Slevin, "Several Factors Contributed to 'Lost' Voters in Ohio," Washington Post, December 15, 2004, p. A01, available at http://www.washingtonpost.com/wp-dyn/articles/A64737–2004Dec14.html.

42. Gregory Korte and Jim Siegel, "Defiant Blackwell Rips Judge; Secretary Says He'd Go to Jail before Rewriting Ballot Memo," Cincinnati Enquirer, October 22, 2004, available at http://www.enquirer.com/editions/2004/10/22/loc_blackwell22.html.

43. Preserving Democracy: What Went Wrong in Ohio, Status Report of the House Judiciary Committee Democratic Staff, January 5,

2005, available at http://election04.ssrc.org/research/preserving_democracy.pdf.

44. Sandusky County Democratic Party v. Blackwell, 387 F.3d 565 (6th Cir. 2004). The Brennan Center simultaneously brought a case on the same subject that was dismissed after the Court of Appeals ruling. See League of Women Voters v. Blackwell, 340 F. Supp. 2d 823 (N.D., Ohio 2004).

45. Justin Levitt, Wendy R. Weiser, and Ana Munoz, Making the List: Database Matching and Verification Procedures for Voter Registration, Brennan Center for Justice, March 24, 2006, available at http://www.brennancenter.org/dynamic/subpages/download_file_49479.pdf.

46. Washington Association of Churches et. al v. Reed Citing 42 U.S.C. § 15483(a)(1)(A)(i), available at http://www.brennancenter.org/dynamic/subpages/download_file_36553.pdf.

47. Gregory Palast, "The Wrong Way to Fix the Vote," Washington Post, June 10, 2001, p. B01.

48. United States Civil Rights Commission, http://www.usccr.gov/pubs/vote2000/report/ch5.htm.

49. Greg Palast, "Ex-Con Game: How Florida's 'Felon' Voter-Purge Was Itself Felonious," Harper's Magazine, March 1, 2002.

50. Gregory Palast, "Florida's Flawed 'Voter-Cleansing' Program," Salon.com, December 4, 2000, available at http://archive.salon.com/politics/feature/2000/12/04/voter_file/print.html.

51. Mary Ellen Klas, Debbie Cenziper, and Erika Bolstad, "State Drops Felon-Voter List," Miami Herald, Sunday, July 11, 2004.

52. Francis X. Clines, "The Election: Unsentimental Education: The Ripe Smell of Political Maneuvering," The New York Times, November 12, 2000.

53. Robert A. Caro, The Path to Power (New York: Knopf, 1982).

54. Hugh Sidey, John F. Kennedy, President (New York: Atheneum, 1964), p. 180.

55. 42 U.S.C. § 1973i(c), (e); 42 U.S.C. § 1973gg-10.

56. Harvard Law Review 127:1144 (2006).

57. See Justin Levitt, "The Truth about Voter Fraud," Brennan Center for Justice white paper (2007), available at http://www.truthaboutfraud.org/pdf/TruthAboutVoterFraud.pdf.

58. Eric Lipton and Ian Urbina, "In 5-Year Effort, Scant Evidence of Voter Fraud," The New York Times, April 12, 2007, p. A1.

59. "City Mislabeled Dozens as Voting from Vacant Lots," St. Louis Post-Dispatch, November 5, 2001, p. A1.

60. John Ferro, "Deceased Residents on Statewide Voter List," Poughkeepsie Journal, October 29, 2006.

61. Commission on Federal Election Reform, Building Confidence in U.S. Elections, September, 2005, p. 89. "As the Report estimates, twelve percent of voting-age Americans do not have driver's licenses. The research collected by the 2001 National Commission on Federal Election Reform shows that between six and ten percent of voting-age Americans do not have driver's licenses or state-issued non-driver's photo ID. That translates into as many as 20 million eligible voters." See also Brennan Center for Justice, "Citizens without Proof," November 2006, which reported a telephone survey of voters and found that 11 percent of respondents lacked a government-issued current ID, a rate that would translate into 21 million voters. Available at http://www.federalelectionreform.com/pdf/Citizens%20Without%20Proof.pdf.

62. U.S. Department of Transportation, available at http://www.fhwa.dot.gov/policy/ohim/hs04/htm/dllc.htm; United States Election Project, George Mason University, available at http://elections.gmu.edu/Voter_Turnout_2006.htm.

63. John Pawasarat, "The Driver License Status of the Voting Age Population in Wisconsin," University of Wisconsin-Milwaukee

Employment and Training Institute, June 2005, available at http://www.eti.uwm.edu.

64. Matt A. Barreto, Stephen A. Nuño, and Gabriel R. Sanchez, "Voter ID Requirements and the Disenfranchisements of Latino, Black and Asian Voters," presented at 2007 American Political Science Association Annual Conference, September 1, 2007.

65. See "Section Five Recommendation Memorandum," Department of Justice memo, September 30, 2005, available at http://www.votingrights.org/news/downloads/Section%205%20Recommendation%20Memorandum.pdf.

66. Purcell v. Gonzalez, 549 U.S. ____ (2006).

67. Alex Keyssar, "'Disenfranchised'? When Words Lose Meaning," Huffington Post, October 22, 2006, available at http://www.huffingtonpost.com/alex-keyssar/disenfranchised-when_b_32241.html.

68. Kristen Mack, "In Trying to Win, Has Dewhurst Lost a Friend?" Houston Chronicle, May 17, 2007, available at http://www.chron.com/disp/story.mpl/politics/4814978.html.

69. Count Every Vote Act: S. 450 (109th).

70. Jonathan Soros, "Vote Early, Count Often," The New York Times, October 30, 3007, available at http://www.nytimes.com/2007/10/30/opinion/30soros.html.

71. See Eric Weiner, "You Must Vote. It's the Law," Slate.com, October 29, 2004.

72. Arizona Voter Reward Act, Ballot Proposition No. 200, 2006.

73. David S. Broder, "Why Vote on Tuesdays?" Washington Post, November 10, 2005, p. A29, available at http://www.washingtonpost.com/wp-dyn/content/article/2005/11/09/AR2005110901650.html.

74. "Reasons for not Voting by Sex, Age, Race and Hispanic Origin," U.S. Census Bureau, February 27, 2002, available at

http://www.census.gov/population/socdemo/voting/p20–542/tab12.pdf.

75. Electionline.org, a website run by Pew Charitable Trusts, keeps track of these laws. See http://www.electionline.org/Default.aspx?tabid=474.

76. Jo Becker, "Voters May Have Their Say before Election Day," Washington Post, August 26, 2004,p. A01, available at http://www.washingtonpost.com/wpdyn/articles/A33796–2004Aug25.html.

77. Center for the Study of the American Electorate, "Making it Easier Doesn't Work," study released September 13, 2004, available at http://www.american.edu/ia/cfer/research/csae_09132004.pdf.

78. Rachel Kapochunas, "Jennings Officially Contests Race in Florida's 13th District," The New York Times, December 20, 2006, available at http://www.nytimes.com/cq/2006/12/20/cq_2056.html.

79. The electoral impact would come because the undervotes were concentrated in Democratic-leaning communities. Testimony of Michael Herron, December 20, 2006, available at http://www.dartmouth.edu/~herron/hearing.pdf.

80. Julie Carr Smith, "Voting Machine Controversy," Cleveland Plain Dealer, August 28, 2003.

81. Robert F. Kennedy, Jr., "Was the 2004 Election Stolen?" Rolling Stone, June 1, 2006, available at http://www.rollingstone.com/news/story/10432334/was_the_2004_election_stolen.

82. http://www.brennancenter.org/dynamic/subpages/download_file_39288.pdf, p. 34.

83. National Institute of Standards and Technology, Draft report, "Requiring Software Independence in VVSG 2007: STS Recommendations for the TGDC," available at http://vote.nist.gov/DraftWhitePaperOnSIinVVSG2007–20061120.pdf; Cameron W. Barr, "Security of Electronic Voting Is Condemned; Paper Systems Should Be Included, Agency Says," Washington

Post, December 1, 2006, p. A1, available at http://www.washington post.com/wp-dyn/content/article/2006/11/30/AR2006113001637.html.

84. http://www.bradblog.com/?p=4888.
85. CalTech/MIT Voter Technology Project, VTP Conference on Voter Authentication and Registration, available at http://www.vote.caltech.edu/events/2006/VoterID/rpt.pdf.
86. Charles Stewart III, "Residual Votes in the 2004 Election," CalTech/MIT Voter Technology Project, VTP Working Paper, Version 2.3, February 2005, available at http://www.vote.caltech.edu/media/documents/vtp_wp21v2.3.pdf.
87. To be more precise, the flaws in voting machines can be fixed by paper trails or by what computer experts call "software independent audit trails." Engineers are continuing to research methods of conducting audits that don't rely on paper, which can be hard for people with disabilities to use, especially the blind. For now, the only available such method is paper—hence the commonly used shorthand.
88. Lawrence Norden et. al, Post Election Audits: Restoring Trust In Election, Brennan Center for Justice and The Samuelson Law, Technology & Public Policy Clinic at the University of California, Berkeley School of Law (Boalt Hall), August, 2007, p. 1, available at http://brennancenter.org/dynamic/subpages/download_file_50227.pdf.
89. According to the American Bankers Association, a conservative estimate for the annual maintenance of the country's ATMs is more than $4.5 billion. Source: http://www.aba.com/NR/rdonlyres/80468433–4225–11D4AAE6–00508B95258D/41737/2ATMFacts.pdf .
90. "Saddam Hussein Wins One-Man Race," CBS News, October 16, 2002, available at http://www.cbsnews.com/stories/2002/10/16/attack/main525770.shtml.

91. See Edmund Morris, Theodore Rex (New York: HarperCollins, 2002), 360–361; for the passage of Roosevelt's reform laws, see more generally, Robert E. Mutch, Campaigns, Congress, and Courts: The Making of Federal Campaign Finance Law (New York: Praeger, 1988), 1–11.

92. Joseph E. Cantor, "Campaign Finance: An Overview," CRS Report for Congress, Congressional Research Service, Library of Congress, July 31, 2006.

93. Michael Malbin, "House Winners Raised an Average of $1.1 Million," Campaign Finance Institute press release, November 8, 2006, available at http://www.cfinst.org/pr/prRelease.aspx?Release ID=102.

94. Center for Responsive Politics, "2006 Election Analysis: Incumbents Linked to Corruption Lose, but Money Still Wins," November 9, 2006, available at http://www.opensecrets.org/pressreleases/2006/ PostElection.11.8.asp.

95. Mark Green with Michael Waldman, Who Runs Congress? (4th ed.) (New York: Dell, 1983), 25.

96. Mark Green, Selling Out (New York: ReganBooks, 2002).

97. Mark Green, "The Evil of Access: Campaign Finance Reform Can Succeed—But Only If the Pressure Stays On," The Nation, December 30, 2002.

98. Simpson quoted in Breaking Free with Fair Elections, Public Citizen et al., p. 6, available at http://www.cleanupwashington.org/ documents/breaking_free.pdf.

99. Greg Giroux, "Top 10 House Fundraisers: Vested Veterans, Vulnerable Juniors," Congressional Quarterly, November 8, 2007, available at http://www.cqpolitics.com/wmspage.cfm?parm1=5& docID=news-000002623778.

100. David Lieberman, "Fight Is on for Campaign TV Ad Dollars," USA Today, August 8, 2007, accessed at http://www.usatoday.com/ money/media/2007–08–08-political-ad-spending_N.htm.

101. Author interview with Rep. Frank, 1982.

102. David Maraniss and Michael Weisskopf, "Speaker and His Directors Make the Cash Flow Right," Washington Post, November 27, 1995, p. A01, available at http://www.washingtonpost.com/wpsrv/politics/special/campfin/stories/cf112795.htm.

103. Nicholas Confessore, "Welcome to the Machine: How the GOP disciplined K Street and Made Bush Supreme," Washington Monthly, July/August 2003, available at http://www.washington monthly.com/features/2003/0307.confessore.html.

104. See Robert Reich, Supercapitalism (New York: Alfred A. Knopf, 2007)

105. Figures on lobbying expenditures from 1999 through 2006 from Congressional Quarterly's Political MoneyLine, available at http://moneyline.cq.com/pml/home.do.

106. Half of eligible Senators and 43 percent of eligible House members became registered lobbyists. See "Congressional Revolving Doors: The Journey from Congress to K Street," Public Citizen's Congress Watch, 2005, available at http://www.lobbyinginfo.org/documents/RevolveDoor.pdf.

107. Center for Responsive Politics, "Pharmaceuticals/Health Products: Long-Term Contribution Trends," available at http://www.opensecrets.org/industries/indus.asp?Ind=H04.

108. John M. Hayes, Healther Walczak, and Allen Prochezko, "Comparison of Drug Regimen Costs between the Medicare Prescription Discount Program and Other Purchasing Systems," Journal of the American Medical Association, July 2005, p. 428, available at http://jama.ama-assn.org/cgi/reprint/294/4/427.

109. William M. Welch, "Tauzin Switches Sides from Drug Industry Overseer to Lobbyist," USA Today, December 15, 2004, available at http://www.usatoday.com/money/industries/health/drugs/2004-12-15-drugs-usat_x.htm.

110. Rockefeller and immunity: Ryan Singel, "Democratic Lawmaker Pushing Immunity Is Newly Flush with Telco Cash," Wired, October 18, 2007, available at http://blog.wired.com/27bstroke6/2007/10/dem-pushing-spy.html. See also Eric Lichtblau and Scott Shane, "Companies Seeking Immunity Donate to Senator," The New York Times, October 23, 2007, available at http://www.nytimes.com/2007/10/23/washington/23nsa.html.

111. Mutch, Campaigns, Congress, and Courts, p. 24–52.

112. Buckley v.Valeo, 424 U.S. 1, 49–50 (internal citations and quotations omitted). For a full critique of Buckley, see E. Joshua Rosenkranz, Buckley Stops Here: Loosening the Judicial Stranglehold on Campaign Finance (New York: Century Foundation Press, 1998), and E. Joshua Rosenkranz, ed., If Buckley Fell: A First Amendment Blueprint for Regulating Money in Politics (New York: The Century Foundation, 1999).

113. Buckley v. Valeo, 424 U.S. 1, 266 (White, J. concurring in part and dissenting in part).

114. Barbara Borst, "Campaign Spending Up in U.S. Congressional Elections," Associated Press, October 29, 2006, available at http://www.usatoday.com/news/washington/2006–10–29-campaign-spending_x.htm.

115. McConnell v. Federal Election Commission, 540 U.S. 93 (2003). The Brennan Center was one co-lead counsel in defending the law before the Court.

116. See Federal Election Commission, Thirty Year Report 3, 2005, available at http://www.fec.gov/info/publications/30year.pdf.

117. Craig B. Holman and Luke P. McLoughlin, Buying Time 2000 (Brennan Center for Justice), p. 45, available at http://www.brennancenter.org/dynamic/subpages/download_file_10670.pdf.

118. Craig B. Holman and Luke P. McLoughlin, Buying Time 2000(Brennan Center for Justice), p. 45.

119. The ruling on requiring separate segregated funds for corporations and unions to make electioneering ads was 5–4. However, the Court ruled by an 8–1 vote to uphold the law's requirement for disclosure of such contributions.

120. After the Court in McConnell ruled that the issue ad provisions were not unconstitutional on their face, the Wisconsin Right to Life committee sued the Federal Election Commission, arguing that it was unconstitutional as applied to their ads. The Court ruled that the McConnell case "did not purport to resolve future as-applied challenges," in Wisconsin Right to Life, Inc. v. Federal Election Comm'n (WRTL I), 546 U.S. 410 (2006). The second Wisconsin Right to Life case then looked at whether in fact the specific ads in question were allowed.

121. George F. Will, "Setback for the Censors," Washington Post, June 28, 2007, p. A25.

122. Wisconsin Right to Life Committee v. Federal Election Commission, 546 U.S. 410 (2006).

123. Richard L. Hasen, "Beyond Incoherence: The Roberts Court's Deregulatory Turn in FEC v. Wisconsin Right to Life," Loyola-LA Legal Studies Paper No. 2007–33, available at SSRN, http://ssrn.com/abstract=1003922.

124. Randall v. Sorrell, 548 U.S. ___ (2006).

125. See the discussion of Nixon v. Shrink Missouri Government PAC, 528 U.S. 377 (2000) in Deborah Goldberg, ed., "Writing Reform: A Guide to Drafting State & Local Campaign Finance Laws" (2004 Revised Edition), Brennan Center for Justice, p. I-12, available at http://www.brennancenter.org/dynamic/subpages/whole_manual_2004.pdf.

126. FEC records available at http://www.fec.gov/press/press2001/0510501partyfund/051501partyfund.html and http://www.fec.gov/pdf/ar04.pdf.

127. Alexis Rice, "The Power of the Internet," Center for the Study of American Government at The Johns Hopkins University, available at http://www.campaignsonline.org.

128. Glenn Justice, "The 2004 Election: Fundraising; Kerry Kept Money Coming with Internet as His A.T.M.," The New York Times, November 6, 2004, available at http://www.nytimes.com/2004/11/06/politics/campaign/06internet.html

129. Rick Klein, "The Note: Obama Arrives," abcnews.com, July 2, 2007, available at http://abcnews.go.com/Politics/TheNote/story?id=3339235&page=1.

130. Frederika Schouten, "Small Donors Can Be Big Deal for Candidates," USA Today, October 18, 2007, available at http://www.usatoday.com/news/politics/election2008/2007–10–18-small-donors_N.htm.

131. David D. Kikrpatrick, "Candidate's Pleased to Remember This Fifth of November," The New York Times, November 6, 2007, available at http://www.nytimes.com/2007/11/06/us/politics/06paul.html.

132. Laura Smith-Spark, "Online Campaigns Bring in the Bucks," BBC News, July 15, 2007, available http://news.bbc.co.uk/2/hi/americas/6293980.stm.

133. I was President Clinton's policy aide on campaign finance reform, and was present for all the discussions described in these paragraphs. See Michael Waldman, POTUS Speaks: Finding the Words That Defined the Clinton Presidency (New York: Simon & Schuster, 2000), 47–55, 71–74.

134. Data on number of contributions provided by the Center for Responsive Politics, as quoted in Kelly Patterson, "Spending in the 2004 Election," in Financing the 2004 Election, David Magelby, et al. editors (Washington D.C.: Brookings Institution Press: 2006), p. 83; data on number of citizens of voting age

provided by Michael McDonald, "Voter Turnout," United States Elections Project website, available at http://elections.gmu.edu.

135. During the three decades with a working presidential public funding system, Carter beat Ford, Reagan beat Carter, and Clinton beat Bush. In the previous seventy-six years, only two incumbent presidents lost: Taft (1912) and Hoover (1932).

136. "CRS Report to Congress: Public Financing of Congressional Elections, Background and Analysis," January 22, 2007.

137. See Herbert E. Alexander, Financing Politics: Money, Elections, and Political Reform, 4th ed. Washington, D.C.: C.Q. Press, 1992, pp. 1, 20. (McGovern spent $30 million in 1972; the first presidential public funding grant was for $20 million, adjusted upward for inflation; see Justin Nelson, "The Supply and Demand of Campaign Finance Reform 100," Columbia Law Review, 2000, pp. 524, 539).

138. "Campaign Finance Reform: Can the Arizona Model Work in CA?" Transcript of Talk with David Iverson, Executive Director of Best Practices in Journalism, July 12, 2004, available at http://www.commonwealthclub.org/archive/04/04–07spitzer-lerner-speech.html.

139. Presentation by Maine Commission on Governmental Ethics, available at http://www.maine.gov/ethics/pdf/maine_clean_election_act.pdf.

140. See presentation available at http://www.njleg.state.nj.us/committees/NJ%20Comsn.ppt.

141. See Jack Newfield and Wayne Barrett, City for Sale: Ed Koch and the Betrayal of New York (New York: HarperCollins, 1988).

142. Telephone interview, November 7, 2007.

143. Elizabeth Benjamin, "Bloomberg'$ Politic$ 101," New York Daily News blog, June 5, 2007, available at http://www.nydailynews.com/blogs/dailypolitics/2007/06/bloomberg_politic_101.html.

144. S.J.Res. 1, June 2007

145. William Safire, Safire's New Political Dictionary (New York: Random House, 1993), p. 279.

146. Lulac v. Perry, Brief of Samuel Issacharoff, Burt Neuborne, and Richard H. Pildes brief of amicus curiae in support of appellants at 2. Available at http://moritzlaw.osu.edu/electionlaw/litigation/documents/Brief_Amici_Curiae_Issacharoff_Neuborne_Pildes.pdf.

147. See Vieth v. Jubelirer, 541 U.S. 267, 274 (2004) (Scalia, A.).

148. Safire, Safire's New Political Dictionary (New York: Random House, 1993), p. 280.

149. See John H. Fund, "Beware the Gerrymander, My Son: Creative Redistricting," National Review, April 7, 1989.

150. Juliet Eilperin, Fight Club Politics: How Partisanship Is Ruining the House of Representatives (Lanham, MD: Rowman & Littlefield, 2007), p. 92.

151. Jeff Toobin, "The Great Election Grab," The New Yorker, December 8, 2003, available at http://www.newyorker.com/archive/2003/12/08/031208fa_fact.

152. Editorial, "Revolt Builds to Force More Competitive Elections," USA Today, August 22, 2005, p. 10A. See also Thomas E. Mann, "Redistricting Reform," The National Voter, June 2005, p. 4.

153. Thomas B. Edsall, "Democrats Hold Edge over GOP in Redistricting; Gains Still Possible for Republicans," Washington Post, December 14, 2001, p. A55.

154. See Brief of American Civil Liberties Union and Brennan Center for Justice at NYU School of Law as amice for appellants in Vieth v. Jubelirer, available at http://www.brennancenter.org/dynamic/subpages/vieth.pdf.

155. "How to Rig an Election," The Economist, April 24, 2002.

156. R. Jeffrey Smith, "Delay's Corporate Fundraising Investigated," Washington Post, July 12, 2004, p. A1, available at http://www.washingtonpost.com/ac2/wp-dyn/A43219–2004July11?language=printer.

157. Available at http://clerk.house.gov/108/01m108.pdf

158. League of United Latin American Citizens v. Perry, 547 U.S. __ (2006).

159. Adam Clymer, "Why Iowa Has So Many Hot Seats," The New York Times, October 27, 2002.

160. See David O. Stewart, The Summer of 1787: The Men Who Invented the Constitution (Simon & Schuster, 2007), page 155–162.

161. Robert W. Bennett, Taming the Electoral College (Palo Alto, CA: Stanford Law and Politics, 2004).

162. Michael Kramer, "Bush Set to Fight an Electoral College Loss," New York Daily News, November 1, 2000.

163. "The Few Decide for the Many, Special Report—Democracy in America," Business Week, June 14, 2004, available at http://www.businessweek.com/magazine/content/04_24/b3887070.htm

164. Fair Vote, "Who Picks the President," available at http://www.fairvote.org/media/research/who_picks_president.pdf. The map, created by Peter Johnson using Fair Vote data, is available at http://upload.wikimedia.org/wikipedia/commons/d/dc/2004CampaignAttention.png.

165. Norman Ornstein, "No Need to Repeal the Electoral College," State Legislatures magazine, February 2001, available at http://www.ncsl.org/programs/pubs/201elec.htm.

166. The Constitution also can be changed through a constitutional convention. However, while the convention can be called with the ostensible purpose of drafting a particular amendment, in

fact its work cannot be limited, as we found out in Philadelphia in 1787.

167. Jonathan Alter, "A Red Play for the Golden State," Newsweek, August 13, 2007, available at http://www.msnbc.msn.com/id/20121791/site/newsweek/.

168. See Hendrick Hertzberg, "Count 'Em," The New Yorker, March 6, 2006, available at http://www.newyorker.com/archive/2006/03/06/060306ta_talk_hertzberg. See also http://www.fairvote.org and http://www.nationalpopularvote.com.

169. See Elena Kagan, "Presidential Administration," Harvard Law Review 2245, 2001, p. 114.

170. Eric Lane and Michael Oreskes, The Genius of America (New York: Bloomsbury, 2007).

171. See Paul Starr, Freedom's Power (New York: Perseus BooksGroup, 2007).

172. Report of the Congressional Committees Investigating the Iran-Contra Affair, with supplemental, Minority, and Additional Views, S. Rep. No. 100–216, H. Rep. No. 100–433 (1987), 435.

173. Vice-President's remarks to the traveling press, December 20, 2005, available at http://www.whitehouse.gov/news/releases/2005/12/20051220–9.html.

174. Frederick A.O. Schwarz Jr. and Aziz Huq, "Where's Congress in This Power Play?" Washington Post, April 1, 2007, p. B01. See also Unchecked and Unbalanced: Presidential Power in a Time of Terror (New York: New Press, 2007).

175. Jack Goldsmith, The Terror Presidency: Law and Judgment inside the Bush Administration (W.W. Norton, 2007), 147.

176. T. J. Halstead, "Presidential Signing Statement: Constitutional and Institutional Implications," Congressional Research Service, updated September 17, 2007, available at http://www.fas.org/sgp/crs/natsec/RL33667.pdf.

177. Report of the American Bar Association Task Force on Presidential Signing Statements and the Separation of Powers Doctrine, August, 2006, p. 14, available at http://www.abanet.org/op/signingstatements/aba_final_signing_statements_recommendation-report_7–24–06.pdf.

178. Thomas Mann and Norman Ornstein, "Steps to Repair the 'Broken Branch,'" Philadelphia Inquirer, December 1, 2006.

179. For a summary of the issue, see Jonathan Hafetz, "Ten Things You Should Know about Habeas Corpus," Brennan Center for Justice white paper, 2007, available at http://www.brennancenter.org/dynamic/subpages/download_file_48810.pdf.

180. The Federalist, No. 84

181. U.S. Const., art. I., Section 9, cl. 2.

182. Hamdi v. Rumsfeld, 542 U.S. 507, 536 (2004).

183. Walter Shapiro, "Rumsfeld Memo Offers Honest Display of Doubts about War," USA Today, October 24, 2003, p. 5A.

184. David Jackson and Kathy Kiely, "Strategy on Terror Suspects Splits GOP; Key Senators Say No to Bush Plan," USA Today, September 15, 2006, p. 1A.

185. Thom Shanker and David Sanger, "New to Pentagon, Gates Argued for Closing Guantanamo Prison," The New York Times, March 23, 2007, p. A1.

186. See generally Aziz Z. Huq, Twelve Steps to Restore Checks and Balances (Brennan Center for Justice, 2007). Since the countries in question do not even abide by their own legal frameworks, such assurances provide "plausible deniability" to the intelligence agency involved without providing any meaningful safeguard against torture. Dana Priest, "Foreign Network at Front of CIA's Terror Fights; Joint Facilities in Two Dozen Countries Account for Bulk of Agency's Post 9/11 Successes,"

Washington Post, November 18, 2005, p. A1; Dana Priest, "CIA Holds Terror Suspects in Secret Prisons: Debate Is Growing over Legality and Morality of Overseas System Set Up after 9/11," *Washington Post,* November 2, 2005, p. A1.

187. Susan Milligan, "Congress Reduces Its Oversight Role," Boston Globe, November 20, 2005, available at http://www.boston.com/news/nation/washington/articles/2005/11/20/congress_reduces_its_oversight_role/.

188. Denis McDonough, Mara Rudman, and Peter Rundlet, Center for American Progress, "No Mere Oversight: Congressional Oversight of Intelligence Is Broken," June 2006, available at http://www.americanprogress.org/issues/2006/06/b1761097.html.

189. The panel was the House Government Oversight Committee. See "Congressional Oversight of the Clinton Administration," Minority staff report, Committee on Government Reform, January 17, 2006, available at http://oversight.house.gov/documents/20060117103516–91336.pdf.

190. Ronald Brownstein, The Second Civil War: How Extreme Partisanship Has Paralyzed Washington and Polarized America (New York: Penguin, 2007), p. 274.

191. See Michael Waldman, My Fellow Americans: The Most Important Speeches of America's Presidents, from George Washington to George W. Bush (Naperville, IL: Sourcebooks, 2003).

192. See Jonathan Rauch, "Divided We Stand," Atlantic Monthly, October 2004, available at http://www.theatlantic.com/doc/200410/rauch.

193. Daryl J. Levinson and Richard H. Pildes, "Separation of Parties, Not Powers," Harvard Law Review 119, pp. 2311, 2374 (2006).

194. Margaret Talev, "Senate Tied in Knots by Filibusters," McLatchey newspapers, July 20, 2007, available at http://www.mcclatchydc.com/homepage/story/18218.html.

195. Gardiner Harris, "Surgeon General Sees Four-Year Term as Compromised," The New York Times, available at http://www.nytimes.com/2007/07/11/washington/11surgeon.html.

196. For discussions of favoritism, see, e.g., Steve Kroft, "All in the Family," 60 Minutes, September 21, 2003, available at http://www.cbsnews.com/stories/2003/04/25/60minutes/main551091.shtml.

197. Jeffrey Toobin, "Is the Justice Department Poised to Stop Voter Fraud—Or to Keep Voters from Voting?" The New Yorker, September 20, 2004, available at http://www.newyorker.com/archive/2004/09/20/040920fa_fact.

198. Carol D. Leonnig, "Political Hiring in Justice Division Probed," Washington Post, June 21, 2007, p.A01, available at http://www.washingtonpost.com/wp-dyn/content/article/2007/06/20/AR2007062002543_pf.html.

199. Charlie Savage, "Missouri Attorney a Focus in Firings," Boston Globe, May 6, 2007, p. A13, available at http://www.boston.com/news/nation/washington/articles/2007/05/06/missouri_attorney_a_focus_in_firings/?page=full.

200. Testimony of Joseph D. Rich, Subcommittee on the Constitution, Committee on the Judiciary, March 22, 2007, available at http://www.nationalcampaignforfairelections.org/page/-/rich%20oral%20testimony%203%2022%20final.pdf (Rich is former chief of the voting rights section.); Rebecca Carr, "Senators Grill Justice Department Official over Voter Fraud Case," cox News Service, June 6, 2007, available at http://www.coxwashington.com/hp/content/reporters/stories/2007/06/06/BC_FIRED_PROSECUTOR06_COX.html.

201. Dan Eggen, "Official's Article on Voting Law Spurs Outcry," Washington Post, April 13, 2007, p. A19, available at http://www.washingtonpost.com/wp-dyn/content/article/2006/04/12/AR2006041201950.html.

202. Karl Rove: TPMuckacker.com, April 10, 2007, available at http://www.tpmmuckraker.com/archives/002982.php.

203. Amy Goldstein, "White House Cites Lax Voter-Fraud Investigations in U.S. Attorneys' Firings," Washington Post, March 14, 2007, p. A06, available at http://www.washingtonpost.com/wp-dyn/content/article/2007/03/13/AR2007031301725.html.

204. Donna Leinwand, "Ex-Prosecutor Says Firing Cleared Way for Another," USA Today, June 5, 2007, available at http://www.usatoday.com/news/washington/2007–06–05-fired-prosecutors_N.htm.

205. Charlie Savage, "Missouri Attorney a Focus in Firings," Boston Globe, May 6, 2007, p. A13, available at http://www.boston.com/news/nation/washington/articles/2007/05/06/missouri_attorney_a_focus_in_firings/?page=full.

206. Craig Donsanto, Federal Prosection of Election Offenses (Washington, D.C.: National Institute of Justice, Sixth edition, 1995).

207. See http://www.talkingpointsmemo.com/docs/schlozman-clarification/.

208. David C. Iglesias, "Why I Was Fired," The New York Times, March 21, 2007, p. A22.

209. See Margaret Talev and Marisa Taylor, "Rove Was Asked to Fire US Attorney," McClatchy newspapers, March 10, 2007, available at http://www.mcclatchydc.com/reports/usattorneys/story/16356.html.

210. Meet the Press transcript, March 25, 2007, available at http://www.msnbc.msn.com/id/17706775/.

211. Dan Eggen and Amy Goldstein, "Voter-Fraud Complaints by GOP Drove Dismissals," Washington Post, Monday, May 14, 2007, p. A04.

212. Michael P. McDonald, "The Competitive Problem of Voter Turnout," Washington Post Think Tank Town, October 31, 2006, available at http://www.washingtonpost.com/wp-dyn/content/article/2006/10/30/AR2006103000712.html.

ACKNOWLEDGMENTS

This book reflects the dedicated work of my colleagues at the Brennan Center for Justice at NYU School of Law, where I have been privileged to work for the past two and a half years. The Brennan Center combines the rigorous research of a think tank with the hard-hitting energy of a public interest law firm. The staff is brilliant, principled, and appropriately cantankerous, and it is a pleasure to work with them.

Frederick A. O. Schwarz, our senior counsel, read the manuscript in several versions and made highly valuable suggestions. Deborah Goldberg, who directs the center's Democracy Program, and her deputies Wendy Weiser (our voting rights impresario) and Laura MacCleery (campaign finance) and Erika Wood (felony disenfranchisement) offered extensive and useful edits. The Center's attorneys and professionals provided expertise at the heart of the book: Justin Levitt (voter fraud and databases and redistricting), Renée Paradis (universal voter registration),

Lawrence Norden (voting technology), James Sample and Ciara Torres-Spelliscy (campaign finance), Myrna Perez (voting purges), and Kahlil Williams (redistricting). Chisun Lee and Andrew Stengel offered excellent editorial guidance. Aziz Huq, who directs the Liberty and National Security Project, and Professor Eric Lane of Hofstra Law School were of invaluable assistance on presidential power and checks and balances, as was Fritz Schwarz. Bethany Foster and Margaret Chen provided capable research assistance. Ceara Donnelly, a gifted Yale Law Student, conducted research on the political reforms of the Progressive Era. Additional research on redistricting was conducted by Jasmine Mahmoud and Annie Chen. Thanks to David Udell, Kirsten Levingston, and Laura Abel for their comments, and Sam Issacharoff and Rick Pildes of NYU for useful answers to substantive questions. Thanks also to Rob Richie of FairVote for insight into the Electoral College.

Three colleagues deserve special thanks. Diana Lee was a dedicated and talented researcher, writer, and organizer. Susan Lehman was a gifted editor, resolving seemingly insoluble structural questions with a deft hand. Erica Payne offered comments, advice, language, and contagious enthusiasm.

It has been a pleasure to work again with Sourcebooks. Special thanks go to my editor, Peter Lynch, and to the CEO of this innovative company, Dominique Raccah. Rafe Sagalyn, my agent, was a wise prod and guide.

Ivan Chermayeff, the renowned graphic designer, and his colleagues at Chermayeff and Geismar were generous to design the book.

The Brennan Center is a unique institution. Many thanks to Board Chair Jim Johnson, as discerning a reader as he is dynamic a leader; Meg Barnette, who kept the organization moving forward during the hectic months this book was being written; David Udell, Kirsten Levingston, and Cathy Mitchell Toren, the managers who make the Center so effective. Dean Ricky Revesz of NYU School of Law is a generous and enthusiastic partner. The law students at the Brennan Center Clinic conducted basic research for many of the lawsuits and reports described here. Our board of directors has been enthusiastic and supportive. Foundations that support the work discussed in this book over the past two years include the Open Society Institute; Carnegie Corporation of New York; the JEHT Foundation; Atlantic Philanthropies; Ford Foundation; Rockefeller Family Fund; John Merck Fund; John S. and James L. Knight Foundation; Joyce Foundation; Tides Foundation; Wallace Global Fund; Omidyar Network; Connect USA; HKH Foundation; Newman's Own Foundation; the Bauman Family Foundation; Dyson Foundation; Educational Foundation of America; Mitchell Kapor Foundation; and Pew Charitable Trusts. Special thanks to Gara LaMarche, head of two generous foundations and a true partner. Many, many generous individuals have supported the Brennan Center. Special thanks for their help over the past year to Patricia Bauman, Gail Furman, Jonathan Soros, Rob Johnson, Rob McKay and the partners of the Democracy Alliance, Jim Torrey, Bernard Schwartz, Brian Snyder, John and Wendy Neu, Jim Johnson and Sigrid Gabler, Ruth Lazarus and

Michael Feldberg, and Susan Sachs Goldman. Thanks also to the leaders of New York's legal and business community who support our organization. The views expressed here, of course, are those of the authors, not all these wonderful supporters.

Colleagues of many years offered advice and guidance as this work came together quickly, including Jonathan Alter, Eric Alterman, Cliff Sloan, George Stephanopoulos, and Mark Green. Rick Hertzberg has been highly persuasive on the Electoral College and much else.

My family was supportive and generous throughout. My parents, Martin and Sandra Waldman, closely read the manuscript and rescued me from many errors. Steve Waldman, Amy Cunningham, Annie Fine, David Frankel, Grant Fine, and Joyce Boudreau were encouraging (and patient as I wound up working through a summer vacation). My children Ben, Susannah, and Joshua, were sharp and loving critics. On this book, as its predecessors, my brilliant wife Liz Fine was the best editor and best friend any author could hope for. (She's now a big macher in New York City government, which makes her time and insight all the more valuable.)

Benjamin Franklin said, "Our critics are our friends, for they show us our faults." I have been lucky to have many friends; the faults are mine.

Michael Waldman
January 2008

ABOUT THE AUTHOR

Michael Waldman is the executive director of the Brennan Center for Justice at NYU School of Law, a leading think tank and advocacy organization focusing on democracy. He was Director of Speechwriting for President Bill Clinton from 1995 to 1999, and was responsible for writing or editing some two thousand speeches, including four State of the Union and two Inaugural Addresses. From 1993 to 1995, he was Special Assistant to the President for Policy Coordination, and crafted the administration's proposal for campaign finance reform. He has been a faculty member at Harvard's John F. Kennedy School of Government, an attorney in private practice, and executive director of Public Citizen's Congress Watch. Waldman is author or editor of books including *My Fellow Americans, POTUS Speaks* and *Who Robbed America?* Waldman is a graduate of Columbia College and NYU School of Law. He lives in Brooklyn, New York, with his family.

The Brennan Center for Justice at New York University School of Law is a non-partisan public policy and law institute that focuses on fundamental issues of democracy and justice. Our work ranges from voting rights to redistricting reform, from access to the courts to presidential power in the fight against terrorism. A singular institution—part think tank, part public interest law firm, part advocacy group—the Brennan Center combines scholarship, legislative and legal advocacy, and communications to win meaningful, measurable change in the public sector. For more information, visit www.brennancenter.org.